HANDBALL

PHYSICAL
EDUCATION
ACTIVITIES
SERIES

Consulting Editor:
AILEENE LOCKHART
University of Southern California
Los Angeles, California

Evaluation Materials Editor:
JANE A. MOTT
Smith College
Northampton, Massachusetts

PHYSICAL EDUCATION
ACTIVITIES SERIES

HANDBALL

MICHAEL YESSIS

California State University,
Fullerton

SECOND EDITION

WM. C. BROWN COMPANY PUBLISHERS
Dubuque, Iowa

Contents

Preface

This book is designed for the college student who wishes to improve the caliber of his handball. Processes involved in the theory and practice of handball from beginning through top level stages of development are presented. The book not only includes explanations of how the game is played but also provides reasons so that you can understand various kinds of play.

The material is presented in clear-cut stages beginning with the fundamentals of handball and progressing to the highest level of skilled participation. Interspersed throughout the book are self-evaluation questions designed to challenge your thinking and to help you evaluate your progress as you move toward top level play. You not only should attempt to answer the printed questions but should pose additional ones as a self check on learning. Since the order in which the content of the text is read and the teaching progression of your instructor are matters of individual decision, the evaluative materials are not always positioned according to the presentation of given topics. In some instances you may find that you cannot respond fully and accurately to a question until all the material has been read more extensively or until you have gained more playing experience. From time to time you should return to such troublesome questions until you are sure of the answers or have developed the skills called for, as the case may be. Handball is a game of strategy—you must *think*.

The Lore of Handball

1

"Handball" is considered to be the oldest of all games played with a ball. As we know it today, the game is of Celtic origin and began in approximately the tenth or eleventh century. It first appeared in Ireland and it is believed to have been carried there from France where it is probable that it had been learned from the Romans. It is known that the Romans played a form of handball in the thermae or baths of Rome, and during the time that France was occupied by the Romans, a game of handball appeared which was known as bare-handed pelota. This game is still played in many parts of Southern France at the present time. Some historians also believe that tennis originated from a form of handball in which the ball was hit back and forth over a net.

During the sixteenth and seventeenth centuries, the game came to be called "Fives" and, according to the first written accounts, became very popular in the Emerald Isle in the mid-nineteenth century when many town and country championships were held throughout the country. It is interesting to note that the courts were from 50 to 60 feet long, 25 feet wide and 30 feet high. The front wall was made of slate and the other walls of cement or smooth concrete. The ball was made of strips of rubber and yarn wrapped around a very small cork center, covered with a fine layer of horsehide and sewn as a baseball. The ball was smaller than a baseball but much faster than the standard handball in use today. Players were allowed to kick the ball and developed much finesse in this skill as most low balls were returned by kicking. This practice can be seen today in Ireland where the players are allowed to kick the ball on the second bounce if it is not returned by hand on the first bounce.

In the recorded history of this game probably the greatest champion was John Cavanagh in the early nineteenth century. It is written that he was superb in all aspects of the game and upon his death there was not one left who was his equal or even second to him in skill. Following Cavanagh in the mid-nineteenth century was William Baggs who introduced more scientific methods of hitting the ball so it would curve and hop. Baggs is often considered the father of modern handball, as his methods of hitting the ball provided the foundation for a new era of handball.

Many great handball players migrated to the United States from Ireland in the late nineteenth century and Phillip Casey is perhaps the best remembered in this country. His enthusiasm and talent did much to stimulate a large following for the sport. In 1887 he played John Lawlor, the Irish champion, for the world championship and a thousand dollars. The match was to be decided by the winner of eleven out of twenty-one games, the first ten to be played in Ireland and last eleven in the United States. The score after the first ten games was six to four in favor of Lawlor, but after returning to this country and playing before large crowds, Casey won seven straight games and thus gained the championship. He successfully defended his title many times before his retirement in 1900, still undefeated. Following Casey was Michael Eagan who won the first Amateur Athletic Union Handball tournament; Eagan therefore was the first official champion of this country.

In the early twentieth century handball developed into two separate games: the one-wall game which can be considered as a truly American version and the four-wall game which was modified in terms of court dimensions and type of ball used. In both games the original hard ball was replaced by a softer ball, a tennis ball with its outside covering removed. Most players wanted a faster ball and this led to the development of a small gas ball; this in turn was modified and became the ball as we know it today which is smaller, heavier, and much faster. Both games require most of the same basic skills and strategies though modifications are made for the different playing areas. It can truly be stated that after a player has participated in either version he usually falls in love with the game. Present day handball players are quick to say that they have yet to know of anyone who, after playing the game, does not like it.

The one-wall game originated along the beaches of New York where bathers found hitting a tennis ball against the open walls of the bath houses with their hands made an excellent game. Because one-wall courts are relatively inexpensive to build when compared with four-wall courts, the number of one-wall courts increased as did the number of new adherents to this game. Bleachers capable of seating two to three thousand spectators were erected and this increased the popularity of the sport. One-wall handball is so common today in New York that almost everyone who grows to manhood there is exposed to the game. This is not to say that it is uncommon in other areas of the country, for the game has spread to all states with added innovations and modifications. In California, for example, a three-wall version is played in some schools and playgrounds. The front wall is the same as in one-wall, but two cut down side walls are added so the more varied front wall play can be seen. A recent innovation in New York combines the one- and four-wall elements of play in a three-wall jai-alai type court. There is a front wall, back wall, one-side wall, and an open side for spectators. Still other courts consist of only a front wall and two full side walls.

The four-wall game, which is now played in most cities, was slower in its growth and gradually spread West from the Eastern seaboard. Credit for this spread is given to the Detroit Athletic Club, where several indoor courts with wooden floors were built and where, in 1915, the first invitational four-wall tournament was held. Fritz Seivered of Cleveland was the winner. Bill Ranft of the Los Angeles Athletic Club won the first A.A.U. National Championship only four years later with the new softer ball. This shows the rapid spread in popularity across the country. Today there is an increasing number of participants due mainly to the construction of new courts in colleges and universities as well as in athletic clubs, YMCAs, recreation centers and other similar organizations.

New York City is considered the stronghold of the one-wall game for both men and women. It is interesting to note that in the one-wall game the service is one of the most important shots and players work for many aces. As many handball players in the East play the one-wall game, they naturally spend a great deal of time developing a strong serve, even if they also play the four-wall game. This may explain why Eastern players put emphasis on the serve and Western players put emphasis on court maneuvering and kills.

Even a brief summary of the development of handball in this country would not be complete without mentioning the work of Robert Kendler and a group of handball enthusiasts. In 1951 they helped form the United States Handball Association (USHA) which is considered the players' fraternity, originated for and by the players. This organization has been responsible for promoting the game throughout the country.

Because of the English and American heritage of handball, the terminology is basic to that used in other sports. You should learn and use these terms properly so that you can talk the game of handball. You should use correct terms so that you and your opponent will clearly understand each other during play and during any subsequent discussion of rules or play.

2 What Is Handball Like?

Handball is one of the simplest and yet most challenging games known to man. The rules are easy to learn and you can quickly understand the game once you see it in progress. Handball may be played by two (singles), three (cutthroat), or four (doubles) players. It may be played on a one-, three-, or four-walled court. There are therefore various types of games possible. Most of the material presented in this book applies to all variations but major concern is with the four-wall game; the latter is the most complex and (although debatable) the most thrilling game.

To start the game one player, the server, stands within the service area, bounces the ball on the floor and, as it rebounds, strikes it with his hand with sufficient force so that it will rebound off the front wall and strike the floor behind the service zone before it strikes both side walls, the ceiling or rear wall. The opponent must then return the ball in such a manner that it will hit the front wall before it strikes the floor. Either hand may be used in hitting the ball; the ball may be struck only once in attempting its return. If the ball is not returned by the opponent, and the ball has been legally served, the server scores one point. During play, if the server fails to return the ball, he loses the serve. His opponent then becomes the server and he becomes the receiver. The first side to score twenty-one points wins the game.

The ball may be played after one bounce or volleyed as it comes off a wall. During play, the ball may strike the side walls, rear wall, and/or ceiling on the rebound from the front wall, or on a return to the front wall. A ball that has bounced twice on the floor may not be played, and when this occurs, either a point is scored for the server or a hand-out is called, depending upon who served the ball at the start of play and who failed to return the ball prior to its second bounce.

In doubles, each partner is given an opportunity to serve before a side-out occurs, except in the case of the initial service when only one partner serves. The purpose of this rule is to help prevent a strong doubles team from winning a game before the opponents have had an opportunity to serve. In doubles, the ball must be returned alternately by the receiving side and the serving side. Either player on a side may return the ball. If two players on the same side return the ball in succession, the result is either a point scored against them or a loss of serve.

4

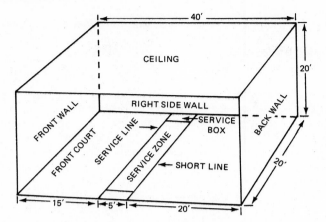

Figure 1—Court dimensions and nomenclature.

The four-wall game is played in an enclosed room in which all walls are playable. It consists of a front wall, two-side walls, a rear wall, a ceiling and a floor. Visualizing yourself enclosed in this relatively small room (40′ x 20′ x 20′), pitted against an opponent with a fast moving ball bouncing in unexpected directions off the floor, ceiling, side, and/or rear wall, can give you an idea of what is involved in the fast game of handball!

To play an effective game of handball it is necessary to have the proper equipment. Because handball requires little equipment, each item becomes very important and at one time or another may be the crucial factor in winning a game.

The basic equipment includes regular gymnasium wear, tennis shoes (sneakers), handball gloves, and an official ball. When choosing your gymnasium wear, it is essential to remember that your shorts and shirts must allow for total movement and must not feel tight. Clothing which restricts arm or leg movement will in turn prevent you from executing a full swing or not allow for the necessary bending, twisting, and running. For maximum leg movement the shorts should be slit up the side while the shirt should be sufficiently loose around the shoulders to allow for a full range of motion. Your shoes should fit well and not be loose. If your feet slip in your shoes you may not only lose a fraction of a second in getting started on a fast side cutting movement but you will also put excess stress on the ankle joint. Blistering of the feet can usually be prevented by wearing two pairs of socks. When you are playing on concrete or on wooden floors for any length of time and find that your legs become excessively sore or begin to ache, you should wear Ripple soled shoes. Because of their greater shock-absorbing ability you will not feel any pounding in the feet and these shoes will help keep the muscles relaxed. You will get greater maneuverability also because of the increased traction created by the ridges on the sole of these shoes.

What are the various types of hinders that can occur in a game and what are the rulings regarding each? Do you call all legal hinders during play? Do you position yourself so as not to hinder your opponent during play?

Handball gloves, which must be worn at all times during play, help to keep the hands free of perspiration and protect them from injury. The gloves are made of leather, horsehide, pigskin, or goatskin. They have a strap, adhesive material, or elastic band to keep them snug around the wrist. It is very important to choose your gloves so they fit very snugly around the fingers and hand. If they are loose, you will have trouble keeping them on after play starts for the gloves will stretch when they become damp from perspiration. If your hands perspire excessively you should wear cotton inserts to prevent the gloves from becoming wet and loose. It is important to rinse the gloves in water occasionally to wash out the salt from perspiration which accumulates in the gloves. If this is not done, the leather will get hard and stiff and will soon crack. When first beginning handball, it is worthwhile to use gloves which are padded in the palm in order to help prevent bone bruises. As your hands become accustomed to hitting the ball, however, you should wear gloves with but a single thickness of leather in order to get better feel and control of the ball. To help prevent bone bruises or hand soreness you should soak your hands in hot water for a few minutes before beginning play. This practice increases circulation in the hand and expansion of the tissues. The expanded tissues then act as a cushion when your hand contacts the ball and protects the underlying bones and blood vessels.

If you use eyeglasses be sure that they are unbreakable and that you have them firmly secured with an elastic retainer so that the glasses will not come off during play. If you do not wear eyeglasses, it is recommended that you use wire or plastic eye guards made especially for handball to help prevent injury to the eye. Getting hit in the eye with a ball traveling at 50 or more miles per hour can be very dangerous, and until you develop court sense, you should protect yourself with some guards.

Aside from the basic athletic wear, the only extra equipment that is necessary is a ball and a pair of leather gloves as required by rule. In four-wall handball, a black rubber ball must be used which is 1⅞″ in diameter and weighs 2.3 ounces.

Of all the various sports engaged in by man, handball probably ranks among the top ten in terms of the number of values that can be derived. There is more all-around body development and physical fitness involved than in most other sports. All parts of the body are used and are essential: both arms and hands, shoulders, waist, legs and feet. It requires a greater amount of energy expenditure than any other individual or dual sport. Consequently one can achieve or maintain a high level of physical fitness merely by playing handball several times a week. Because handball requires quick mental responses to constantly changing game situations, it is also valuable in developing fast decision and reaction abilities.

The most outstanding factors which can be developed by participating in handball are muscular strength and endurance, cardiorespiratory endurance, agility, flexibility, decreased movement time, symmetrical development of the body, improved timing and neuromuscular coordination. Handball is especially effective in maintaining a trim waist because it requires so many flexing and twisting movements. This strenuous and exciting sport requires and leads to the all-around fitness which is advocated so strongly by top medical and physical education personnel. Total fitness is essential for successful living. This condition allows an individual, regardless of his occupation, to perform his daily tasks with much greater ease and effectiveness.

Participation in handball helps to develop the lungs, heart, blood vessels, and probably even more important, the ability of the body to re-create and/or strengthen its restorative processes and metabolic functions. These factors are responsible for new cell and tissue growth, the prolongation of youth, and keeping all body systems functioning at a very high level. Participation in handball exercises all body systems which in turn adapt to the great demands placed upon them, thus strengthening them. Of very great importance, after finishing a game of handball, the player feels mentally and physically relaxed and satisfied.

Handball is now popular with many businessmen who have little spare time and are under tremendous mental strain. Through this sport, these men find relaxation and maintain top physical ability, both necessary for effective job performance. Handball is also played by people in diverse occupations; astronauts, for example, participate in handball to maintain their physical condition. Handball is played by athletes and coaches during the off-season in order to maintain fitness, improve quickness of movement, and/or to develop strategy similar to that required in their respective sports.

The sport is played by people of all ages for it is possible to vary the intensity and frequency of participation according to objectives, interests, and needs. Nor is handball limited to men; there are many women who play four-wall handball and a larger number who participate in single-wall handball.

Although handball has gained tremendously in popularity during the last decade, growth in this country has been relatively slow. Perhaps one reason is that very few people have been able to watch a game in progress because spectator facilities are generally lacking. This situation is now being remedied, however, for an increasing number of handball courts are being constructed today which provide open or glass enclosed galleries for spectators; these are placed high in the rear or in the side walls.

There never has been a controversy about one thing: experienced players wholeheartedly agree that once you have participated in handball you will continue to come back for more, be it for fun and enjoyment and/or for the biophysical values to be derived!

3 Essential Skills

It is important that you have correct body, arm, and hand position in order to be able to hit the ball well. These prerequisites will aid you in achieving effective ball contact, sufficient force, and the control necessary for accurate placement. If you concentrate only upon hitting the ball, without regard for the necessary form, the result will be frustration. Your shots will be weak, wild and will usually result in easy returns for your opponent.

For executing most shots your hand should be held in a relaxed position with your fingers bent slightly in a cupped position. Your fingers should not be held together tightly because this will cause a tight wrist; the latter makes impossible the complete flexibility needed for most hits. The ball should be contacted with the base of the fingers and the upper palm of the hand. The ball is slung or thrown from this contact position rather than just being hit by your hand. As a beginner you may experience some difficulty with this action but do not be discouraged; ability can be developed in a relatively short period of time if you practice correctly. Most beginners find, while learning, that many of their hits are made in the palm of the hand or off the fingers. This is normal as most hits will inadvertently be contacted in these areas while eye-hand coordination is developing. After some practice, however, you will find it easier to contact the ball on the base of the fingers and you will develop the feel of throwing or slinging it. (See Figure 2 for good and poor ball contact positions.)

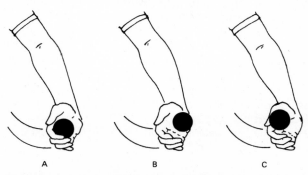

A   B   C

Figure 2—Ball contact positions. (A) Good position. (B, C,) Poor positions.

In preparation for returning the ball stand relaxed facing the front wall with your arms at ease. As your opponent prepares to begin his serving or hitting action, you should assume the "ready position," a position from which it is easy to move in any direction while preparing for the return hit. To assume the ready position bend forward slightly from the waist and unlock the knees. Do not bend the knees excessively or go into a deep crouch as this will cause you to lose time when going into action. Raise both arms slightly so that your forearms are almost parallel to the floor and the elbows flexed to form a 45 to 90 degree angle. Feet should be shoulder distance or more apart. There are many slightly different ready positions but the basic concepts of each are the same. Many times the ready position which you assume will be determined by the play going on or by your physical condition at that moment. (See Plate 1 and the first frame of Plate 5 for examples of the ready position.)

Plate 1—Examples of the ready position.

In the ready position your weight should be borne in the middle of your feet and not on the balls of the feet. This will keep you more relaxed and not create extra tension in the muscles which extend the knee joint. After your opponent hits the ball and you see that you will have to move forward, or forward and to the side, immediately shift your weight on to the balls of the feet so that you can move as quickly as possible in the desired direction. If you see that you will have to go to the back corners or to the back wall straighten the body thus enabling you to move more quickly to the rear.

When getting ready to hit the ball, you should always be in a position to swing your arm freely without feeling cramped or tight. When you are in a relaxed position with your arms free to swing, you will have time to think where you want to hit the ball, and even more important, you will have effective control of your hits. Facing the side wall is the best position for most shots. When hitting a right-handed shot, you should therefore be facing the right-side wall with your left hip pointed toward the front wall. The opposite is true for a left-handed shot. Your position is probably the key point for you to remember as it will determine the outcome of your shots in most instances.

Hitting the Ball

The actual swing and hit is a highly coordinated neuromuscular act requiring precise timing of powerful muscular contractions in a proper sequence of actions to produce maximum velocity of the hand and fingers. The force and momentum generated by each joint is transferred to the next adjacent joint culminating in your hand, thereby achieving maximum force and speed. In other words, you are trying to get a summation of internal forces working from the large musculature of the leg, hips, trunk and shoulders out to the smaller muscles of the arm and hand.

All the actions involved in hitting the ball can be broken down into four phases: the preparatory or backswing phase; the power or forward-swing phase; the contact phase, when the ball is in contact with the hand; and the concluding or follow-through phase. Although each phase is distinct, there are overlapping portions of each in the total swing action. Also, modifications of the basic motions in each phase take place when hitting underhand, sidearm or overhand but the same basic principles are applicable.

Preparatory Phase—In the preparatory phase backswing movements take place in order to prepare for the forward-swing actions. From the ready position this entails turning into a side-facing position while still maintaining a slight crouch, shifting your weight to the rear leg, rotating the hips and shoulders to the rear, bringing the arm back to a position in line with or behind your shoulders, bending the elbow of the rear arm, and hyperextending (cocking) the wrist while keeping the fingers slightly curled but relaxed. (See Plate 2.) All these actions are done sequentially

Plate 2—The backswing.

beginning with the foot and working up to the hand. For example, if you are a right-handed player, you would execute the following sequence of movements to hit a ball for which you have to move in on. You start the action by turning the right foot so that the toes point toward the right-side wall. (See Figure 3-B.) (If you had to back up for good positioning, the footwork outlined in Figure 3-A should be used.) As this action is being completed push off the left foot by extending the ankle and knee joints and abducting the left hip joint in order to shift the weight to the rear right leg. To abduct the hip joint move the hips over the rear leg while keeping the feet and head and shoulders in their original position. Rotate the hips to the rear and then the shoulders followed by the bent arm and then cocking the wrist. As these actions are taking place you must keep looking at the ball.

It is good practice, when trying for correct body position, to anticipate where the ball will be when you will be making contact. Read the path of the ball and then position yourself accordingly. Most often, especially in singles play, this will necessitate taking several steps to be where the ball will be and then going into all the hitting actions.

Power Phase—The power phase begins prior to completion of the preparatory movements. As the arm and hand are being brought to the rear, forward weight shift occurs by the same actions as previously described but with the right leg. Start the movements by stepping in a direction toward the oncoming ball. (See Figure 3-A, B.) For the most efficient hit you should step out at a 45 degree angle; that is, toward the front and side walls. Toes of the left foot should also point in this direction. On a fast ball coming right at you step directly toward the front wall, and if the ball is going deep, you should step directly toward the side wall.

In order to step out you must extend the ankle and knee joints and perform right hip abduction to shift the weight forward. This action, known as "stepping into the ball" or "getting your body into the hit" is very important

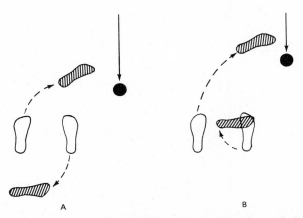

A   B

Figure 3—Footwork patterns. (A) When the ball is deep. (B) When the ball is "shallow."

for the production of power. As you shift your weight forward, it is vital that the rear foot maintain contact with the floor until the ankle and knee are fully extended. If not, the momentum generated by the body will be lost. To absorb the weight of the body coming forward, the left leg, after making contact with the floor heel first, flexes at the ankle, knee and hip joints. The amount of flexion is determined by the amount of weight transference and how low the ball is. The length of the stride is likewise determined by the height of the ball. If the ball is to be contacted low, a long stride is taken; if the ball is to be contacted waist or chest high, a moderate step forward is taken.

As forward weight shift is being completed, forward rotation of the hips occurs followed by forward rotation of the shoulders. It is important that your hip and shoulder rotation be maximal in the hitting position that you assume prior to beginning movement of the arm. Only in this way can the muscles be "put on stretch" which is necessary if the muscle group is to have a powerful contraction. Once the shoulders have rotated so that the upper body is facing the front wall, the arm begins its forward action with the elbow leading and the forearm and hand still to the rear. As the elbow comes in line with the body, elbow extension begins but the wrist remains cocked. As the hand lines up with the elbow and the body, wrist action occurs. (See Plate 3.) There are several distinct types of wrist action, the use of which is usually dictated by the stroke being used, position of the ball in relation to the body and by what effect you wish to impart to the ball. Although wrist action begins prior to ball contact, the main actions occur during contact and are therefore explained below. (See Plates 5-9 and look at all the frames up to the moment of contact for visual descriptions of the above explanations.)

Contact Phase—Initial contact with the ball occurs when the ball is in line with the hips or in line with the center of the body after the body has been transferred forward. In other words, in line with the body when the body is in its final position ready for contact and not where your body was when you first started the backswing movements. The ball remains in contact with the hand for about 1/80 of a second, and when it leaves the hand, it is in line with the forward leg. During this contact time, the ball is compressed and immediately expanded, which puts it into flight; this adds to

Plate 3—The swing.

the force gained from your moving hand. With such a short period of contact any wrist action that occurs must be very fast. This is why before attempting to impart any "stuff" to the ball you should have the necessary muscular development.

During contact, if you want to hit the ball without putting spin on it, you should flex the wrist and fingers. To do this, keep the palm of the hand perpendicular to the floor during contact. If you want to impart side spin to the ball so that it rebounds sharply to the right or to the left as it comes off the front wall, you should come across the ball from behind to the right or to the left. The ball should be spinning clockwise on a vertical axis (when viewed from above) in order to rebound sharply to the left, and spinning counterclockwise if it is to rebound sharply to the right. If you come across over the ball during contact, you will impart top spin which will cause the ball to rebound higher off the front wall, and if you come across under the ball during contact, you will impart backspin to the ball which will make it rebound lower off the front wall. However, every time you put spin on the ball, it will travel slower; to be most effective in your strokes you should not constantly use only one kind of wrist action. The path of your hand during ball contact should remain level or in a straight line if the hit is being directed upward or downward. As you try these different wrist actions, you will discover that the left and right arm must be used in order to produce all the different kinds of spin.

When hitting the ball, you should hit it hard; do not hit easy except occasionally or when the play calls for it. Many players when first learning a skill that requires speed and accuracy mistakenly believe that they should hit easy until they can control the ball and then try hitting harder. However, it has been proven that speed and accuracy are developed most effectively by practicing both at the same time so this is what you should do.

Follow-Through—As soon as the ball leaves your hand, the concluding or follow-through phase movements begin. This part of the swing is as important as any other phase even though the ball has already left the hitting hand. If you stop the swing at the moment the ball leaves your hand continuity of your swing will inevitably be disrupted. When you stop the swing too soon, the muscular braking action causes a decrease in the force and momentum that has been generated; in addition, in stopping the swing the hand will not be in the desired position and this will cause the ball to travel in an unpredictable direction.

In the follow-through all body movements follow the hand. As the hand follows the ball for a short period of time the arm comes forward followed by the shoulders, hips, rear leg and foot until you finish up in a position facing the front wall prepared to assume the ready position. After the handball has left your hand, your swing should be continued until it stops of its own accord. This will occur naturally and you should not strive to finish up in a particular position advocated as being the most worthwhile. Every player will finish his stroke differently although they will usually look similar. (See the final frames in Plates 5-9 for pictures of the follow-through.)

The most important phases of the swing are the power and contact phases. It is not critical that you look a particular way in the preparatory or follow-through phases except as how position relates to what you do during the power and contact phases. For most effective hits, however, it is imperative to execute all phases of the swing to the fullest extent. This includes the backswing when the body is wound up and the arm brought back; the forward swing where power is generated as you get your body into the hit and unwind with strong hip and shoulder rotation; the contact phase when speed and spin is imparted to the ball; and the follow-through to insure a smooth continuation of movement.

In practice, and much of it is required, it is not necessary for you always to hit a ball to develop this swing. You may go through the motion by thinking of the separate phases and then imagining the execution of the total move. Learning involves the development of correct pathways from your brain to your muscles. As practice of these motions continues, the pathways become stronger. You will find yourself becoming more relaxed at this time and experiencing less fatigue for you will have eliminated unnecessary tension and unnecessary movement. When your swing becomes smooth and well coordinated, it will no longer be necessary for you to think of what you have to do. When you have learned the swing, it will have become an automatic act.

After hitting the ball, you should immediately return to the correct court position in anticipation of the return which will be made by your opponent. You should not look back to see where you hit the ball or to see if your opponent is going to return it. You should not look back, as compelling as the desire may be, because to do so puts you into the dangerous position of getting hit in the eye by the ball. This point must be remembered in order to avoid serious damage to your eyes. After hitting the ball, your main responsibility is to get into position for the return which in itself precludes any possibility of watching the ball.

The Basic Strokes

The foregoing analysis and description for hitting the ball applies to all the basic strokes. Except for minor modifications in your body and arm positions, you should use the same fundamental swing while executing all of the strokes described below.

The Underhand Stroke—The underhand stroke is used in many shots which are hit very low, approximately knee level or below. The underhand stroke is not often used by many top players as it is more difficult to direct the ball on a level or downward plane. Also it is not possible to get maximum power because the amount of hip rotation and elbow extension is limited. However, there are a few outstanding underhand hitters who have great shoulder strength and so use this stroke effectively. Underhand strokes are most often used for low placements on the front wall when hitting in front court and for high placements from back court although this is very difficult to control. The underhand stroke is also used quite often when fast play does not permit sufficient time to get into a side-facing position, usually when up close to the front wall.

In the full underhand stroke your body is crouched with sufficient lean of the upper body and bend in the knees to insure proper hand contact with

the ball. Your arm is kept relatively straight (but not stiff) on the backswing until it achieves extension in the vertical plane. It remains thus on
the downswing and follow-through, keeping close to your body when the
hit is made. Your hand, which circumscribes an arc in the vertical plane, is
kept in a slightly cupped position with the wrist firm throughout the swing.
As proficiency in this stroke increases, you should add a wrist snap in order
to impart greater force to the hit or to put spin on the ball. To do this, cock
the wrist on the backswing and vigorously flex it at the moment you sling
the ball. (See Plate 4 for an example of the underhand stroke.)

*Plate 4—The underhand stroke. Notice the good forward weight shift,
shoulder rotation, and eye contact. The ball is contacted on the heel
of the hand which in this case was necessary in order to keep the
ball low as initial contact was too far out in front.*

The Sidearm Stroke—The sidearm is the most important stroke in handball. It is used in the majority of shots which are hit approximately between chest level and below knee level when in a crouched position. In preparation for the hit the forearm should be brought back fairly level to the floor with the elbow flexed. As you step into the swing, have the weight shifted forward and have the hips and shoulders rotated to the front; the arm begins to come forward with the elbow leading and the hand cocked. As the elbow approaches the middle of the body, some extension takes place; the amount depending upon how far the ball is from the body and if spin is to be put on the ball. For maximum power and with little or no ball spin the elbow should be fully extended during the contact phase. If the ball is fairly close to the body (approximately one to two feet away), the elbow will extend proportionately. If you want to put spin on the ball, the elbow should remain flexed. You should take a full follow-through as this will almost automatically place you in the ready position for the next shot. (See Plates 6, 7 and 9 for examples of the total swing.)

The Overhand Stroke—When the ball is above your head, use the overhand stroke. To execute this stroke raise your arm up and back in a vertical plane as you shift your weight to the rear by dropping the rear shoulder after assuming the side-facing position. To do this, merely laterally flex the spine (bend over sideways). This action is the same as when throwing a baseball or football. As the forward swing begins (after the weight has been shifted forward and the hips and shoulders have been rotated forward), the elbow should lead as it does in the other two strokes. If the ball is well above your head, your arm should straighten prior to hitting the ball. (See Plate 8.) If the ball is at approximately eye level, your arm should remain flexed until after you have made contact. After the hit is made, the arm is extended and should be straight on the follow-through.

At times it is advantageous to hit the ball so that it will travel in a horizontal plane toward the front wall with great speed. The ball may also be hit in a downward direction, but this is more difficult to control, and you should avoid it until you have mastered the high and level hits. When contacting a very high ball, direct the ball so that it will hit on the ceiling close to the front wall or high on the front wall. You should take a full follow-through and execute the entire swing in a vertical plane. To help insure a high hit assume a position under the ball; this will require additional bending of the body toward the rear.

Combination Strokes—As the ball cannot always be hit in the ideal position, with respect to distance from the body and height at the moment of contact, variations or combinations of the basic strokes are sometimes used. If the ball is a few feet away from your body and below your knees, for example, you should use an underhand-sidearm stroke. If the ball is high but away from your body, a sidearm-overhand stroke should be used. In general, the farther the ball is from your body the more the sidearm stroke should be used, combined with the underhand when the ball is quite low and with the overhand when the ball is fairly high. (See Plate 5 for an example of the sidearm-underhand stroke.)

It is essential that you learn the basic strokes before you can hope to

Plate 5—The sidearm-underhand stroke. Notice the good body move-
ments, footwork, and eye contact up to the moment of ball contact.
Taking his eyes off the ball at the last moment resulted in poor ball
contact position with the ball hitting on the fingers.

achieve any degree of proficiency with the various combinations. In order to master the basic skills it is very important that you assume the correct position on each occasion before attempting to hit the ball. It is therefore necessary for you to learn to judge where the ball will be. Judgment and anticipation are very important aspects of handball and should receive your attention from the beginning.

Use of the Basic Strokes

The Service—As in most other dual sports the serve is often the determining factor in losing or winning. It is therefore most important to have a strong, effective serve. All of the basic strokes are utilized in serving, consequently the effectiveness of the serve depends upon the skill with which you can execute the basic strokes. As your skill increases, your serves will become stronger. During the serve you have the advantage of having ample time to think of which serve to use; where to hit the front wall; and what speed or force will be necessary in order to achieve your purpose, i.e., to score, or at least to hit the ball in such a manner that your opponent will have difficulty in returning it. You should look at the serve not merely as a means of getting the ball into play but as an important shot requiring your deliberate and calculated thought. Various shots you can execute on the service follow.

THE POWER SERVE. The power serve, which utilizes the sidearm stroke, is one of the most common and effective serves. You hit the ball hard so that it travels to the rear corner; your opponent will then be forced to make his hit after the ball rebounds off the floor for there should not be any rebound off the rear wall. If the ball is hit higher than anticipated, it may still be effective if it is placed close to a side wall or if your opponent has to play it from a crowded position in the rear corner. In each case you will have inhibited your opponent's swing.

To execute this serve well, you should be positioned fairly close to and facing the side wall in a deep crouch, bending at the waist and knees so that your hand is below the level of your knees. This will help insure a low hit on the front wall and will increase the possibility of getting your full body momentum into the shot. The ball should be released from your hand at a low height so that it will not rebound high, and the hit should come when the ball is momentarily stationary, at the top of the bounce. The ball should be bounced away from the body so that the arm can swing freely and not be impeded. Remember that you will be stepping into the hit; so the ball must be bounced to a position where it will line up with the hips after the weight has been shifted. (See Plate 6 for the power serve.)

For greater power, you should take two steps prior to dropping and hitting the ball. It is also important to snap your wrist vigorously as you make contact with the ball in order to impart greater speed to it. To keep the ball low it is necessary to have a long, low follow-through. To hit the ball to your opponent's left arm, you should serve the ball from the right side of the service zone; you should aim at center or left of center on the front wall so that the ball will rebound toward the left rear corner. (See Figure 4 for description.)

THE LOB SERVE. The lob serve, effective as a change of pace, is almost the extreme opposite of the power serve. The ball is hit easily and makes a high ballistic flight to the rear corner. For a lob serve you should aim to hit high on the front wall using an underhand swing that contacts the ball low on the initial bounce, or using an overhand swing that contacts the

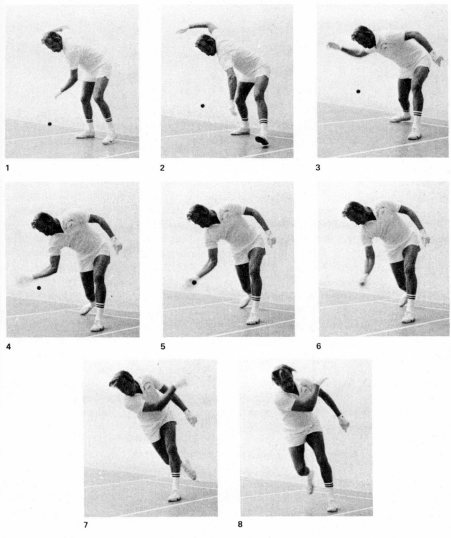

Plate 6—The power serve.

Which position is most effective when playing singles: A, B, C, or D? Why should you strive to maintain this position? How could you get your opponent out of this spot so that you could assume it? After you decide on a particular shot can you anticipate the shot and placement that your opponent will strive for?

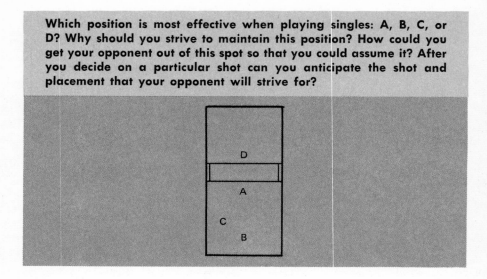

ball high over the head from a high initial bounce. The underhand stroke is, however, easier to control. Both techniques are effective but the high hit ball of the overhand stroke will carry higher for a longer time and will not describe as curved a path as it will in the underhand stroke. The ball in either hit should have sufficient impetus to just reach the rear wall after rebounding off the floor. It will then drop sharply. The receiver will usually swing impatiently at this seemingly easy floating setup or else will get caught in a position where he cannot use a complete arm stroke in his return because the ball is close to the side wall. You will find this serve especially effective when your opponent is keyed up and ready for a fast moving ball.

To execute a lob serve you should position yourself in the center or slightly on that side of center in which you want to hit the ball. You should hit the ball in such a manner that it will rebound directly toward the rear corner. The ball should hit the floor in mid-court and then bounce into the corner. (See Figure 4.) Some players stand very close to the side wall when serving the lob, but it takes greater control in hitting the ball so that it will not hit the rear side wall and bounce away where it becomes a potentially easy shot to return. You can see that with these two serves a variety of returns are possible and for these the server should always be prepared. The ball can be returned on a fly, half volley (immediately after striking the floor), bouncing off the floor, or rebounding from the rear or side wall. You should also be aware that for every serve on one side of the court there is also an identical serve on the other side of the court. Each should be attempted, and mastered if possible, for a large and effective repertoire of serves is essential to a top performer.

THE DIAGONAL SERVE. As proficiency is gained in the power and lob serves, you should then begin to develop the diagonal or "Z" serve. In order to gain the maximum power and control necessary for the proper execution of this serve, the sidearm stroke is used although the underhand stroke can also be used. In order to hit the ball to the left rear corner you should position yourself close to the left side wall in the service zone, facing toward the right front corner. You should then strike the ball so that it will hit the front wall approximately two to four feet from the right side wall, depending upon which hand is used in serving. Upon rebounding from the front wall, the ball develops counterclockwise spin; this spin is further increased as the ball immediately comes off the side wall in the front corner. The ball should then bounce in the back court. Because of the existing spin, the ball, upon hitting the left side wall, will rebound almost parallel to the rear wall. If the rebound is very close to the rear wall, as it should be, then this serve becomes very difficult to return. (See Figure 5.)

The diagonal is most effective when hit low and hard enough so that the spin which is necessary will be generated when the ball rebounds out of the front corner. It can also be executed from a high bounce in which case an attempt is made to hit the ball high on the front wall in the same pattern as with the underhand stroke but at a different height. In this case the ball is not hit hard, however, and because of its slower speed the ball will drop sharply in the back court close to the rear wall. It is therefore difficult to return.

Because of the sharp rebound angle of the low, hard-hit diagonal serve, it is very difficult to return when it bounces off the floor. This makes it necessary for most players to try to play it off the side wall or possibly off the rear wall. It should be remembered that the server is out of position when executing this serve, so as server you should move immediately into the middle of the court after hitting the ball. You should hit the diagonal serve to either corner, depending upon your opponent's weaknesses.

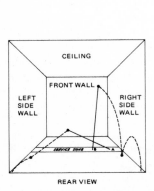
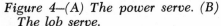
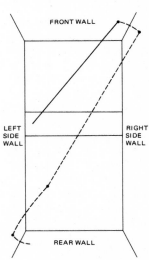

Figure 4—(A) The power serve. (B) *Figure 5—Top view diagonal "Z"*
The lob serve. *serve.*

THE ANGLE SERVE. Almost all serves are angle serves, for the server always attempts to place the ball where it will be very difficult if not impossible to return. One of the most effective spots toward which to serve is the rear corner, close to the wall. There are several additional serves, difficult to return, which are used in attempting to achieve this placement. Most of these serves can be hit with the underhand, overhand, or sidearm strokes, the sidearm stroke being preferred. For these serves the server stands in the same position as indicated for the preceding serves; this likeness adds a desirable note of deception.

One of the most effective angle serves is one that is hit low and hard, hitting the front wall a few feet on the far side of the center of the front wall so that it will hit the side wall a few inches from the floor just beyond the short line (the back boundary line of the service zone which divides the court into two equal halves). The ball will rebound off the side wall very low and fairly sharply so that it is difficult to return; if the opponent gets his hand on the ball, his return is usually soft and quite high. An ace, a ball that eludes the receiver, will usually occur if the low, hard-hit ball strikes the junction of the side wall and floor at the same time. This is called a *crotch* shot. If the ball hits floor and wall simultaneously from a very low angle, it will not rebound sufficiently high to allow its return, or it may rebound at an unpredictable angle. (See Figure 6.)

You should be able to serve the ball at an angle so that it will hit the front wall approximately four to five feet high and then rebound off the side wall at approximately this height just beyond the short line. The ball will then bounce deep in the back court and carry to the rear wall toward the far corner where it will rebound to the opposite side wall, but not very sharply. The ball will have a tendency to hug this side wall especially if it has lost most of its original momentum, and will drop sharply because of the spin generated. You should remember that every time the ball hits a wall it loses some speed. In this serve the ball hits three walls after rebounding off the front wall so it is slowed down considerably. This serve, commonly known as the *scotch serve,* is difficult to return if properly placed. To play the ball after the bounce, the receiver must retreat deep into the back court; this action usually puts him off balance. You should not hit this serve too high or too hard for if you do it will come out of the corner in a way that makes possible an easy return. (See Figure 7.)

OTHER SERVES. Another effective serve is the *straight corner* shot. Your initial position in the service zone should be about six feet from the side wall. You should hit the ball at about knee height, approximately three or four feet from the corner on the front wall on the same side so that it will rebound from the floor deep in the back court hitting the rear wall six to twelve inches away from the corner. Upon rebounding off the rear wall, the ball should travel very close to the side wall. Your opponent will usually be hesitant about taking a full swing on his return for fear of injury. If he does hit it, his angle of return will be very small; as a result his return will be weak. If the ball comes straight off the back wall rather than going into the corner, it will be an easy shot to return.

The same reasoning can be applied to the lob serve. The ball in this

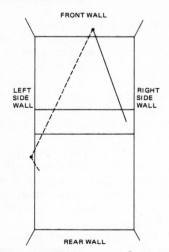

Figure 6—Top view low angle serve.

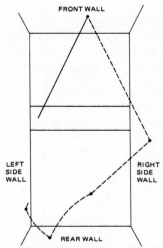

Figure 7—Top view angle serve (Scotch serve.)

case will drop sharply as it remains close to the side wall after rebounding off the rear wall. Both the straight corner and lob shots, however, are vulnerable as the receiver has a chance to return the shot before the ball ever reaches the rear wall. He may choose to volley the lob shot, and he may return the low shot off the bounce before it hits the rear wall. Either response may give him an advantage: by getting off a quick return he may catch you off balance.

SERVICE STRATEGY. You should strive for a high degree of effectiveness in one or two serves but should not rely solely upon these. If you do, your opponent will be able to prepare himself because he will know what to expect. It is important for the same reason to change both the speed and the area to which the ball is aimed. Changing the speed is very important for this throws off your opponent's timing. If you vary only the type of serve, never its speed, your opponent will quickly adjust to this speed and have greater success in retrieving all balls regardless of variation in their location on the floor or wall.

Try various serves, various speeds, and various placements. If you follow the general guidelines presented here you will have some degree of success even from the very first attempts. Precise accuracy will not be achieved at the very beginning for accuracy requires much practice. However, if you direct most of your serves into the rear corners where they will be difficult for your opponent to return, mix up your serves in both placement and speed, and have one or two well-developed serves to use in the "clutch," you will be well on your way to becoming a top level player.

The Playing Shots—After the ball is served you must use basic shots to score a point. The most lethal of these is the kill shot, followed by the passing shot, the ceiling shot, and the lob. Although the kill is the most effective offensive shot, it should be remembered that any one of these shots may be equally effective in achieving the major purpose: to hit the ball away from your opponent so that he cannot return it or to draw him out of an advantageous court position. To execute these shots successfully, there is a prerequisite: the proper positioning of your body so that your entire swing can be performed as previously described. The most frequent error made by beginners is neglecting to position themselves for the next shot, so their shots are weak and/or wild. The forthcoming shot looks so easy that they relax; as a result the shot must be attempted from either a flat-footed position or by rushing at the last minute. You should position yourself so that you can return the ball efficiently and effectively.

THE KILL SHOT. There are many variations of the kill shot but they all have the same end result: the ball stays so low after rebounding off the front wall that it is virtually impossible to return it. Also it may *roll out* in which case there is no bounce as the ball rolls out on the floor after rebounding off the front wall. The kill is the most spectacular of all shots; it leaves your opponent helpless even when he sees it coming.

In the early learning stage, the kill shot is very difficult to execute consistently but it should always be attempted if your position is correct and the ball can be contacted low. The only time you should violate this rule is when your opponent is in an excellent position to play your shot. Kill shots may be played from different heights and from various positions on the court, but you should concentrate on contacting the ball very low. This is the basic rule which most beginners tend to disregard as they are usually too anxious to hit the ball and so do not wait for it to drop sufficiently before attempting the kill shot. You must have patience and wait for the ball to drop. You should attempt a kill shot only when you have an easy play and are set for it. Remember that there is some spot in the court where the ball will be in a position for the kill shot.

The simplest of the kill shots is the *straight kill* or the *front-wall kill*. You can execute this shot from various positions—close to the front wall, in mid-court or near the back wall—depending upon the position of your opponent. As the name implies most straight-kill shots come into and rebound in a straight line from the front wall; the straight kill can be used effectively when driven down a side wall or in a line away from where your opponent is standing.

The most effective kill shot is the *corner* or *two-wall kill*. The ball should first strike low on the side wall, very close to the front wall and then strike the front wall. After hitting low on the side wall, it rebounds in a downward direction so that when it hits the front wall it is very close to the floor and has a good possibility of rolling out; but if it does not, the ball will still have a reduced rebound off the front wall and floor and this makes it most difficult to return. To hit the front wall first and then the side wall is also effective, but because of the opposite spin generated, the ball will rebound higher off the floor thus giving your opponent more time to play it. Also, in the corner kill when the ball strikes the side wall first and then the front wall it is traveling in a direction away from your opponent, making it more difficult to return. When the ball hits the front wall first and then the side wall, it is traveling more in a direction toward your opponent, which makes it easier to return.

Can you execute several angle serves so that the ball is directed into the rear corners? serve a hard ball so that it strikes the side wall very low just beyond the short line?

To keep your kill shots low it is important that you assume a deep crouch for the hit. If you are close to the front wall, your hand should be in an open cupped position to enable you to get more force and spin on the ball so that it will drop lower on contacting the walls. Quick movements are necessary in executing the corner kill when you are positioned forward in the front court. In this shot, rather than directly facing the side wall, you should stand at an approximately 45 degree angle to the side wall so that your forward hip is facing the corner where you intend to hit the shot. In other words, you stand parallel to the line of flight of the ball, or when hitting the ball a line drawn across both toes should be parallel to the ball's line of flight.

The kill shot is usually hit hard to help eliminate any chance of a return but occasionally it may be hit easily. This is known as the *soft kill*. This shot should seldom be used and then only when your opponent is in the back court and has little chance of returning the ball. The stroke is executed in exactly the same manner as the regular kill shot except the ball is hit easy so it dies soon after hitting the corner. Almost all kill shots should be used as offensive shots either to score a point or win the service from your opponent. A possible exception is the kill from the back wall which is usually a defensive shot but it can result in an effective offensive hit.

BACK WALL PLAY. Playing the ball off the back wall will probably be one of the most difficult skills for you to master. Back wall play requires considerable concentration and the ability to position yourself correctly for the shot and not run or chase after the ball. It is essential that you keep looking at the ball while it is in flight and turn to face the back wall. This position will enable you to move easily in any direction in order to make the return. In general, you should turn your body in the same direction that the ball is traveling and be prepared to pivot as you get ready for the hit so that you assume the all important side-wall facing position. The pivot also gives you added momentum which is needed to achieve the greater power necessary to cover the distance to the front wall. As the ball rebounds off the rear wall, you should be positioned sufficiently far away from the wall to allow the ball to drop to knee or below knee height before hitting it. You should begin your backswing as soon as you begin to pivot, and as the ball approaches your body, you step forward with the foot nearest the front wall and rotate the body in exactly the same manner as previously described in hitting the ball. The arm then begins its downswing behind the ball and makes contact as soon as the ball is in line with your face, low to the floor. A long, low follow-through should then be taken to help insure that the ball stays low near the floor. (See Plate 7.)

At times, if it is a fast moving ball coming out of the rear corner, you may not have sufficient time to position yourself facing the side wall. In such cases you must rely upon body pivot to carry your body around sufficiently so that the ball is sent in a forward direction. Your body must twist

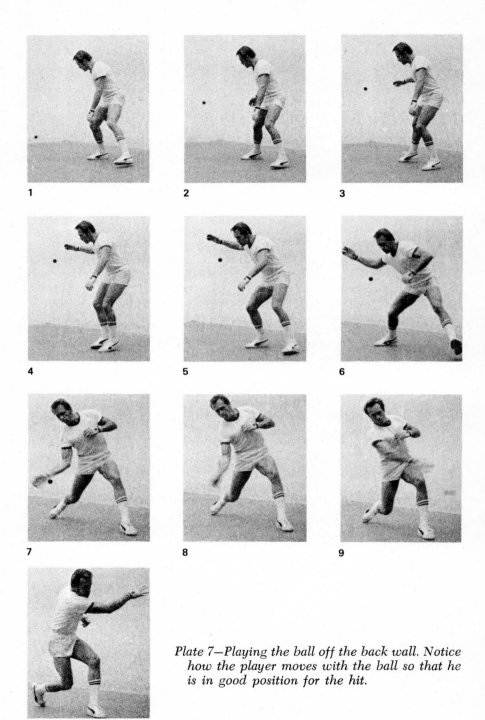

1   **2**   **3**

4   **5**   **6**

7   **8**   **9**

10

Plate 7—Playing the ball off the back wall. Notice how the player moves with the ball so that he is in good position for the hit.

around during the hit. As the hit is completed, however, you should be completely pivoted so that you finish in a position facing the front wall.

THE PASSING SHOT. Probably the most frequently used shot is the passing shot, commonly known as the "workhorse of handball." The shot is relatively simple to execute as it can be hit with an overhand, sidearm, or underhand stroke and, as the name implies, is merely a straight shot driven past your opponent. The ball which should strike the front wall first is hit at such an angle that it carries past your opponent and beyond the short line hitting either the side wall or the floor and without reaching the rear wall. If the ball does reach the back wall, it should be so low that it cannot be returned before it bounces twice. A ball hitting several side walls will be expending its speed; this will give your opponent more time to reach the ball.

To be most effective the passing shot should be hit very hard, a carom shot, so it will have sufficient speed to go by your opponent before he can reach it. This shot should be used whenever your opponent is caught out of position. It is much more difficult to pass your opponent when he is in center court position or to try passing him when he is positioned behind the service line. In these cases the ball should be hit so that it will remain very close to the side wall. This is a more difficult shot. Some of the best passing shots are hit with a bent arm overhand stroke; this is where the most power for this shot can be created. It is also the fastest shot, as the ball travels in an almost level plane though with some downward direction which helps increase the speed. The passing shot is used most often when your opponent is in the front court, close to the front wall.

THE CEILING SHOT. The ceiling shot is another very effective shot that is relatively easy to execute but used far too little because it is more difficult to control in speed and direction. It is a stroke that can be used both offensively and defensively. In this shot, when you are in the center court, the ball should be hit upward with an overhand swing so that it hits the ceiling approximately two to three feet away from the front wall. The ball should contact the ceiling farther back from the front wall if you are hitting from the back court. When the ball hits the ceiling, it develops backspin, and when it hits the front wall, it drops sharply and rebounds very high off the floor. It is most difficult to return this rebound since the ball then will drop in the back court where it will probably hit low on the back wall and drop sharply to the floor. If the ball hits high on the rear wall it will once again drop sharply, making it more of a struggle to return. An advanced player usually will be able to kill the ball coming off the back wall following a ceiling shot provided it is not hit into the corner close to the side wall and is at least above his knees on the rebound.

In order to execute this shot effectively the ball should be contacted high so that a full overhand stroke can be used. (See Plate 8.) The ball should be hit with moderate force since a hard hit ball will carry high onto the back wall making a return possible. The main objective is to have the ball drop into the corner or hit so low on the back wall that it will not rebound.

Plate 8—The ceiling shot. Notice the good hip and shoulder rotation and how the elbow leads followed by strong elbow extension.

The ceiling shot is used to make your opponent move out of front court position so that you can regain the advantage. As an offensive shot the ball is hit off the ceiling at such an angle that when the ball rebounds off the front wall and floor it will stay very close to the side wall and/or fall into the rear corner. This shot is especially difficult to return if it is hit into the corner where the return involves using the weak arm in executing an overhand stroke.

THE LOB SHOT. In general, if the ball is hit high, as in a lob or ceiling shot, it should be returned with another high ceiling shot. The lob shot should be used only when you want to gain the time necessary to take the offensive position. In executing the lob the ball should be hit easily, striking high on the front wall. The hit should direct the ball to the rear corner so that the rebound off the floor will give the ball just enough impetus to reach the rear corner very close to the side wall. The same techniques used in the ceiling shot can be employed to execute this shot.

THE FLY HIT. At times you may find it necessary to volley the ball, that is, hit it on the fly. This is a difficult shot to master and you should use it only when you have an easy opportunity, preferably when maintaining your position in front court. Hitting the ball on the fly should be attempted more often in doubles when you are in good front-court position and do not wish to go on the defensive by running into the back court. In singles you should attempt a volley when you can catch your opponent off guard with a quick passing shot. If a better shot can be executed by letting the ball bounce before hitting it, you should strive for this. If you try for too many volleys you will invariably deny yourself a chance for a kill shot. A volley can be executed with the ball at the height which calls for a kill, passing or ceiling shot. In all fly ball hits you should go through the same motions as described for execution of other shots but greater concentration is needed to help insure proper timing. (See Plate 9.) Do not attempt to volley when you are off balance or when you have to over-stretch or lunge for the ball. Also, you may find that there is insufficient time to execute all the necessary body movements. The ball will be traveling toward you with great speed, consequently you need meet it with only firm forward motion in order to return it with ample force.

THE PICKUP. When in front-court position and the ball is hit at you hard, fairly low and bouncing right at your feet, you should immediately prepare for a *pickup* (hitting the ball immediately as it rebounds off the floor). You should remain facing the front wall and use an underhand stroke, keeping the arm straight and the wrist firm. The sidearm-underhand stroke should be used when you have to move to the side to get to the ball. It is very important that you keep your eyes constantly focused on the ball during flight and while making the hit, for the slightest deviation is sufficient to throw your swing off. As a result the hit will be weak or you will miss it altogether.

The pickup is used many times as a defensive shot in which case the main purpose is merely to return the ball to the front wall; this is necessary especially when off balance. When used as an offensive shot the ball is hit with the intent of making low placements on the front wall or in the corners; it is also effectively used as a passing shot when your opponent is out of position.

THE WALL "HUGGER" SHOT. Many times in a game situation you will find that the ball is traveling right next to the side wall, hugging the wall, and must be returned from this close wall position. In order to hit the ball you should slide the hand alongside the wall. The little finger side of the hand should be in contact with the wall. (See Plate 10.) Do not take a full swing or swing so that the fingers will hit the wall. In so doing there is a good chance that the fingers will be severely injured.

Plate 9—The fly hit.

Plate 10—The wall "Hugger" shot.

ADDITIONAL HINTS. It is essential that you master the fundamental elements of the swing before you can expect to execute successfully the various serves and shots which comprise the sport of four-wall handball. Always think immediately of turning your body so that you will face the side wall to be in a position to take a full smooth swing. Think in terms of a split body. If the ball approaches on your left turn to use your left hand and if the ball approaches on the right side move to use your right hand. In executing your shots do not move in a direction to favor one arm over the other.

During the swing think of shifting the weight forward, rotating the trunk and shoulders into the shot as well as bringing the arm through its full range of motion. Keep your eyes on the ball throughout the swing and completion of the hit in order to gain accuracy in direction. Contact the ball with a slightly cupped hand at the junction of the palm and fingers and get the feel of snapping the wrist in the throwing, slinging motion of the hit. Remember, the elbow leads in almost all strokes.

These essentials should be kept in mind during the execution of the various shots which utilize the underhand, sidearm, overhand or a combination of these strokes. Learn to react immediately to a situation with a definite stroke. In the game situation begin to think about which shot will be most advantageous. In other words, use strategy: plan ahead rather than just hitting the ball and hoping it will score a point. Always try to hit the ball away from your opponent. Think of the shots that will force your opponent out of position—including the kill, passing, and ceiling shots. Be in the right place at the right time. Do not jeopardize your position by being on one side or the other thereby allowing your opponent to execute a passing shot or any other equally effective shot. Always get ready prior to the hit if you hope to have perfect or near perfect execution of the return of a shot. As mastery of these basic strokes and shots is developed you will then be ready to go on to the more advanced shots which are very necessary when playing top level handball.

4 Progress Can Be Speeded Up

Proper physical conditioning can speed up learning and development. General exercises which develop muscular strength and endurance, agility, speed, flexibility, circulatory and respiratory endurance, and neuromuscular coordination are helpful in producing the all-around physical capabilities necessary to play the game well. Once you acquire these necessary requisites you will find that you will receive greater satisfaction and enjoyment from playing the game. Naturally your enthusiasm for handball will increase as you (1) find you have greater power in your serves and shots, (2) can move faster to reach the ball, (3) can change directions and position yourself for a shot quickly, (4) have increasing amounts of energy which makes it possible for you to play longer and at a higher level, (5) find you have the ability to make quick and accurate decisions, and (6) find you are able to evaluate various playing situations correctly and can carry out your plans. You should remember that the difference between winning and losing is many times accounted for by differences in fitness.

General Conditioning

Your general physical conditioning should consist of various localized and total body activities. Included in the localized activities should be exercises to increase flexibility (range of motion) and exercises to increase muscular strength and muscular endurance.

The most popular local exercises which you should do to develop strength and endurance of the major muscles involved in arm movement are push-ups and pull-ups. To improve wrist action do wrist curls with the palm up, turned to the left and turned to the right. To develop the muscles most involved in hip and shoulder rotation perform bent knee sit-ups with a half twist, single and double leg raises from a hanging or supine position so that the toes touch the contralateral hand and back raises with a half twist. Leg squats, toe rises and side bends with the weight on one leg should be executed for development of the muscles used in quick movements and for getting your body into the hit respectively. To gain flexibility in the shoulder joint do forward and rear-arm circles, and for the ability to get low you should do the slow hamstring stretch in a sitting position.

The most beneficial total body activities are running long distances at a moderate pace and short sprints at maximum speed. These activities will help develop circulatory and respiratory endurance as well as some of the above physical qualities. To develop agility you should do side, front, and rear cutting movements while keeping your eyes fixed on a target.

No set number of repetitions or amount of resistance can be recommended here. Such decisions will depend not only upon your initial physical condition but on your level of aspiration. What are your objectives? Also, the activities described are by no means the only ones that you can or should do. If you have any questions or need further information, consult a professional physical educator.

THE WARM-UP. Before beginning to play a game you should make sure that you are well warmed up and have practiced the various hitting coordinations. This will help prevent injury to the muscles and will allow you to start your game at a high level. You should not begin to play a game until you feel loose and can hit the ball well, even if your opponent is urging you to a quick start. To begin your warm-up, start with calisthenics designed to stretch the muscles and connective tissue around all the joints. Include such exercises as arm circles, side stretching, deep knee bends, front and side splits, trunk bending and twisting, and running in place. You should then slowly begin throwing the ball with underhand, sidearm, and overhand strokes, using both arms.

After you have been playing the game for a period of time and have some mastery of the various shots, you should increase your warm-up time and make it more specific. Throw for special shots such as throwing the ball in the back corners with a return hit to the front wall; throwing against the back wall for a straight kill shot; hit straight and corner kill shots from a position in front court; hit fly balls; hit ceiling shots and execute different serves.

The warm-up should be varied especially in those situations when you are having trouble with a particular shot or if you need more stretching of certain muscles. Once completed you should be ready to play.

SUGGESTIONS FOR PRACTICE. The key to a strong game is practice. Practice constantly repeating the strokes and shots until you are able to perform them automatically. To many people, practice seems to imply drudgery but remember that there are many ways to practice, which are both interesting and challenging. Practices, however, should be performed diligently with maximum effort for there is no other way in which learning and development can take place.

When practicing it is important to know what you are practicing for and to know how to perform the skill. You should keep in mind a specific stroke or shot that you want to improve or learn and direct your practice toward this end. Almost every stroke or shot can be practiced either individually or with a partner merely by throwing the ball in a way to duplicate the situations that arise during a regular game.

In the very first stages of learning it is worthwhile to practice the basic strokes without regard to where the ball is going. If you are having trouble integrating the body parts in the swing, you should then practice the stroke without the ball. To develop the basic stroke and eye-hand coordination, it is advantageous to position yourself facing the side wall; bounce the ball to the desired position and height and then execute the stroke being worked on. After success with this practice, throw the ball to the front wall so that it will rebound to the desired spot and once again go through the same action. Once mastered, assume a ready position, throw the ball to the front wall, turn for correct hitting position and repeat the stroke. Then practice by throwing the ball short and/or long from the ready position; so you must move up or back to get into position before repeating the entire swing.

Practice of this nature is progressive. You add a new element to those already learned each time you practice. As you begin to play some games you will very soon discover your weaknesses and your practice then should be directed to correct these weaknesses, one at a time. Remember that a good player will always play to your weaknesses, and if he has good placements, you may find that your greatest weakness is the left arm if you are right-handed so specific attention should be directed toward its improvement. One of the best ways to start is to get the feel of throwing the ball left-handed in an underhand, sidearm, and overhand motion. As the total body coordination is developed, you should begin hitting the ball in a progressive manner as already described. In the beginning and later stages at least three-fourths of your practice time should be spent working with the nonpreferred arm until it can function as effectively as the other.

To practice the various shots when working alone you should throw the ball in a manner to imitate the effect you desire. For example, to practice the back wall shot, stand facing the back wall and throw the ball against the wall so that it will rebound to you at various heights in order that you can practice returning the ball with a kill or a passing shot. To practice back wall corner shots do the same thing: throw the ball either on a fly or on a bounce into the corner and then return the ball with different shots in different directions. As you become more proficient, throw the ball hard against the front wall so that it will rebound in the back corner for the same desired effect.

Before attempting the ceiling shot you should first throw many ceiling balls from the back court in order to acquaint yourself with the different angles of rebound which come with varying speeds. You should then throw the ball easy and high on the front wall so it will rebound high in the back court where you are positioned and then execute the ceiling shot. This exercise can be alternated with back wall play; then you can either hit the ball for a ceiling shot or let it rebound off the rear wall and attempt a kill shot.

For practice of kill shots you should position yourself in front center court or in closer, and work on hitting a kill both from a dropped ball and on a rebound from the front wall. For corner kills assume the same court position but hit for the corners, trying to hit the side wall first. This should be done from a straight throw to the front wall and from a throw into the corner as you progress. As your proficiency increases in killing the ball from a position close to the front wall, you should gradually increase the distance away from the front wall. Similar situations can be set up for practice of other shots. After skill is developed in the basic strokes and shots, practice time should be devoted to development of fast footwork and the

Do you think ahead one or two shots when trying to get your opponent out of position? Can you effectively change the speed of your hits and use different shots for a change of pace? Do you work for a kill or winning shot or do you just keep the ball in play?

ability to change directions quickly while moving. Trying to maintain a rally from center court position is a very effective drill for practicing these elements; major concern should be given to proper positioning and movements rather than how effectively you hit the ball. As footwork is developed more attention can then be directed to the execution of the shots.

Serves should be practiced individually with attention focused on where the ball hits the front wall, where the ball rebounds and with what effect. You should look to see where the ball goes so that in a game situation you will know where the ball is and not have to look back after executing the desired shot. In all of these practices both arms should be used.

If you practice with another person, the same drills can be executed. One player should set the ball up and the other should try for the return. This arrangement can be very beneficial if the one who is doing the setting can also detect errors and point them out to you. In this way any tendency to pick up bad habits will be diminished and learning will be enhanced. You should have expert instruction in the basic skills as well as having your mistakes pointed out and corrected.

It is very beneficial to practice drills for placements and passing shots. Have the receiver stand in front of you in center court position with the ball. Let him throw the ball to the front wall so that it rebounds to you; then you try to pass him on either side. Analogous setups can be arranged to practice kill, ceiling, and lob shots. As proficiency increases, the service and return can be practiced by two players. The server should announce that shot and you should prepare for it with a specific return. In time this practice can be carried on without advance notice of the shot to be hit. You can also play out the point after a legal serve and service return.

In another variation the receiver should assume the ready position in center court and his partner should throw the ball simulating a particular shot; the receiver should then try to return the ball. The point may be played out if desired. If both of you have weak left arms you should play a game using only the left arm for all serves and most shots. Right-handed hits should be taken only when the ball is close to the right side wall. This is probably the best practice to force yourself to use the weak arm and speed its development.

Practices should approximate the game situation as closely as possible. Many other variations can be used as development of the basic fundamentals is continued. For example, to practice the volley, kill, and passing shot, rally with a multitude of strokes using a side wall as the front wall and the opposite side wall as the back wall. Because of the shorter distance thus provided, the play is very fast; this will help develop your reaction time. Very important in all practices is analyzing what you are doing so that you can determine if you are utilizing all the principles of proper stroking and hitting. If you are cognizant of what you are doing, you will be able to correct yourself. This is an important step toward continuous improvement, especially when your instructor is not present. Equally important is to be able to develop the ability to think ahead, to determine the possible offensive and/or defensive shot that can be used and to anticipate the shots that may be hit to you in various situations. In the more advanced stages it is important that you be able to analyze your game in order to determine your weaknesses and to analyze your opponent's game to determine his strong and weak points so you can build your game accordingly.

Competition—In order to improve steadily and keep your game on a high level, you should play as much as possible. With sufficient playing you will be able to maintain proper timing and keep your skills at their maximum peak. Playing in many tournaments is also very important even if you do not aspire to become a Class A player. In tournament play you must play your best game; you are forced to try for precise placements and execution of the various shots. Of at least equal importance is the fact that during tournament play you have an opportunity to learn from your opponent, especially if he is a better player and has some strokes or shots that you feel would be effective in your game. This is one of the reasons why you always should try to play with someone who is more skilled, as you can pick up many pointers if you are alert and have learned to analyze.

You can also gain much from watching top level performers in various tournaments. When you are a spectator you are more relaxed and can more readily follow the play. You can observe the shots used most often by the better players and also note when they are used. You can pick up many new ideas especially in terms of strategy and the finer points of play from top competitors. If this information is applicable, you should incorporate it in your game so that you will constantly be improving and strengthening your game.

Tournaments are not just for champions. There are many levels of tournament play available in areas where handball is played. Tournaments are held quite often by Athletic Clubs, Ys, recreation departments, colleges, and universities. If you live in an area where there are several handball centers, you can probably find a tournament beginning every month or so. There are usually three categories of play in most tournaments: Class A for advanced players, Class B for intermediate to advanced players, and Class C for beginning to intermediate players. If it is a large recognized tournament, and you win in either class C or B, you must then play in the next higher bracket. In this way all players have a chance to keep advancing but yet play on a level consistent with their ability. For national tournament play you should be a class A player and a very good one at that.

Most tournaments are held on weekends so everyone is given a chance to play, even if occupied with work or school during the week. Occasionally you may find a local club tournament held in the evenings. If it is a large tournament, it will usually include both singles and doubles. To learn of these tournaments you should keep in touch with your local club or wherever handball is played.

Information about regional and national tournaments as well as local news can be obtained in *Ace,* the national magazine devoted to handball.

Included in this magazine are articles on various aspects of handball, pertinent information on playing the game and results of handball tournaments throughout the country. This magazine is considered a player's magazine but individual subscriptions can be obtained by writing to the United States Handball Association Magazine, 4101 Dempster Street, Skokie, Illinois.

The USHA holds a number of national handball tournaments throughout the year and conducts many exhibition tours throughout the country. The USHA is mainly responsible for the national tournament and aids also in governing the various regional competitions. Some of the finest tournaments throughout the country are conducted by the many private athletic clubs and YMCAs located in almost all large cities. There are many invitational meets with other clubs throughout the year and everyone who holds membership in the club is eligible to play. These and other clubs have played a major role in maintaining and fostering the growth of handball for many years.

GENERAL REMINDERS. Following are some of the more important points that you should remember. They are general reminders or hints to playing a better game. They have been derived from the more common errors committed by beginners and if constantly recalled may keep your mistakes at a minimum.

1. In practice and during warm-up do a great deal of throwing, especially with the weak arm.
2. Keep your eye on the ball as you prepare to hit it and while you are hitting it.
3. Step into the ball and take a full swing.
4. Split your body in half; if the ball approaches on the left side take it with the left hand; if on the right side use the right arm. Use both hands.
5. In back wall play, swing in the direction that the ball is traveling when it rebounds off the back wall.
6. If the ball is high, hit it high, if the ball is low, hit it low.
7. Learn the kill shot and keep trying it. However, do not kill every shot; mix your shots.
8. Let the ball come to you; do not rush your shots.
9. Aim for a specific spot on the wall, do not just hit and hope. Make a mental picture of the path the ball will take, especially on your returns.
10. Use the side walls and ceiling as much as possible in your hits.
11. Maintain center court position before and after a shot.
12. In doubles, as soon as your partner's serve passes the short line, get into position to hit the return shot by your opponents. Never be caught in a position with your back against the wall unable to swing at the ball.
13. Remember that speed is a great asset but control will win more games.
14. Develop effective serves; each service should be difficult to return. When in doubt, serve to the corners and put spin on the ball.
15. Always be ready; think ahead, anticipate.
16. Try all the shots; practice them and do not be afraid that you will not be successful.

5 Better Players Master These Techniques

General Characteristics

There are a few general characteristics which immediately distinguish the better player. He executes his shots efficiently and the results are effective. His movements are smooth, well-coordinated, and automatic. He anticipates the play and reacts immediately to quickly changing situations. Not only is his footwork automatic but he is almost always in the right position to execute his shots. Instinctively he turns his body to face the side wall, shifts his weight into the shot, strokes, anticipates his opponent's hit, plans his own response, and moves to his ready position. All these decisions and actions appear to be automatic for the better player; they occur as soon as he sees the ball coming off the front wall and often well before. The ability to anticipate, however, is at least partly the result of experience. Thinking in advance not only allows the good player to put pressure on this opponent but also gives him the advantage of having time to conserve his energy between shots.

ADVANCED SHOTS AND STROKES. The better player is able to get into proper position for each shot because he follows the ball longer; consequently he has a good idea where the ball will rebound and so can prepare for it. Remember that you should never look back to see where you hit the ball so that you will not get hit in the eye. When you develop sufficiently, you will be able to tell if there is a possibility for a fast return and not look back. On all other shots you should follow the ball until it is about to be hit. Though you do not watch the actual hit, you should take notice of your opponent's body position in relation to the ball so that you can calculate where and with which shot the ball will be hit. By drawing an imaginary line across the toes of both feet when the receiver is ready to hit the ball, you can determine the direction in which your opponent is aiming. You also can take notice of his general stance: if he is in a deep crouch, look for a low shot; if on a high bounce he dips his rear shoulder, prepare yourself for a ceiling shot; or if he is standing fairly straight he is probably planning a passing shot. Once you have "read" your opponent's intention, no anticipatory move should be made until the actual swing is begun, for your opponent will change his shot or direction very quickly if he sees you moving in anticipation of his shot. Take precautionary protective measures by keeping your hand or arm in front of your eyes to block the ball if it is hit directly at you.

Can you hit a kill shot from deep in the back court? from a back wall rebound? from a rear corner rebound? when the ball rebounds off the rear wall from a ceiling shot? Do you execute the straight kill shot or the corner kill shot? Can you execute these kill shots with either hand?

The Wrist Snap—In situations requiring immediate action, you should use only the wrist snap with little or no body action; this shot should be used only as a last resort when the ball is in tight and you have no chance to employ a more effective shot. The wrist snap requires fast and vigorous contraction of the hand flexors in order to impart sufficient power and speed to the ball.

The Hops—A very effective shot used by advanced players is the *hop*, known also as a hook, reverse hop, or natural hop. In a hop, as the name implies, the ball upon hitting the floor from the front wall hops to either the right or left. In order to produce a hop it is necessary to place spin or "English" on the ball. The ball should strike the front wall at such an angle that will cause it to rebound directly to the floor, at the receiver's feet; the spin then causes the ball to hop to one side or the other. The ball should not hit the side wall or back wall after hopping from the floor, as it will lose its spin and come out as an easy setup.

When serving a hop shot to break to the left (the natural hop), you should stand a little to the right of center in the service zone, facing the right side wall. The stroke is made in practically the same manner as the power serve except that you ulnar flex and supinate the right hand. In other words you move the hand so that the little finger side of the hand moves toward the forearm as the palm of the hand turns toward the ceiling and right-side wall. As contact is made with the ball by your cupped hand, the ball is rolled across your palm and leaves from the index finger and thumb. Your elbow remains close to the body throughout the hit and the hand is sliced across and under the ball, as in a chopping action. This cutting action on the ball creates much side spin or clockwise spin on a horizontal axis when viewed from behind. If the ball had clockwise spin on a vertical axis, it would break sharply to the left upon rebounding from the front wall. The ball must spin on a more horizontal axis; this spin is not affected when the ball hits the front wall but upon striking the floor it causes the ball to hop to the left. To achieve the most effective hop, it is important to hit the ball so that it travels and rebounds parallel with the floor. The ball should hit the front wall a little to the left of center so that it rebounds sufficiently far from the side wall in order that it does not strike it after hopping. To return the hop, try to play it on the rebound off the hop; if you cannot do this probably no other play will be possible.

For a less drastic hop to the left but an equally effective service you should stand on the left side of the service zone close to the left side wall. You should use the same stroke in hitting the ball but should direct the hit to the front wall at a greater angle so that the ball will rebound toward the right corner. When the ball hits the floor, instead of going into the side wall as it appears to be going, it hops slightly to the left as it strikes the floor and remains close to the side wall until it drops into the corner.

To produce the *right* or *reverse hop,* spin opposite to that used for the left hop must be applied to the ball. To do this you should pronate and radial flex the hand. In other words turn the hand so that the thumb side moves toward the forearm and the palm turns toward the body and the floor and make contact with the ball when it is farther away from your body. You should hit the ball on the outside and as contact with the ball is made your hand wraps around the ball in an up and over motion. After initial contact is made, the ball should be allowed to roll across the fingers and palm of your hand leaving at the junction of the little finger and lower edge of your palm. As the ball rolls across your hand, counterclockwise spin is imparted to the ball on an almost horizontal axis, which in turn causes the ball to bounce sharply to the right upon hitting the floor after rebounding off the front wall.

The same basic serves can be achieved with a right hop as with a left hop by reversing the initial starting positions. For the straight right hop serve you should stand a little to the left of center in the service zone and hit the ball low and a little to the right of center on the front wall. For the corner shot you should stand on the right side of the service lane and hit the ball left of center on the front wall so that it will go toward the left corner. As the ball rebounds from the floor it will hop slightly to the right and travel almost parallel to the side wall.

You should use the same body motion for both the left and right hops in order to prevent your opponent from knowing which hop is coming. You should perfect both hops; otherwise your opponent will soon expect only one and be able to prepare himself for it. It is not essential to hit the ball very hard in order to achieve sharp breaking hops, as perfect timing and contact are more important in imparting the necessary spin. The longer the hand remains in contact with the ball the greater the spin, provided the hand action is correct.

Hops are a valuable asset both in your serves and in the passing shot. The receiver who is chasing or charging a shot will usually be thrown off balance when the ball takes a sharp hop to one side. Sharply breaking hops, however, require very vigorous movements of the forearm; therefore it is very important that you be sufficiently warmed up and loose before attempting these shots. They require good muscular development also.

The Kill Shot—One of the most spectacular skills of the top player is the kill shot, which he can execute from any place on the court. He uses any stroke or combination of strokes when executing the kill shot although the sidearm is favored. The top player uses the kill shot often but only because he has the shot well developed and is confident that his shot will be effective.

In addition to the straight front wall and corner kill shots the skilled player also kills the ball on the fly and on the half volley. The *fly kill* is a very difficult shot to execute as great control and accuracy are required. You should not attempt this shot unless you are in a good position and your opponent is either off balance or in the back court where it will be difficult for him to return the ball. The *half volley* or *pick-up kill* is also very difficult to execute because it is very fast and requires maximum concentration. In both of these kill shots an underhand or sidearm stroke is used and to be most effective the ball is hit to the corners, striking the side wall first. It must always be hit low. On the fly kill you should let the ball drop until it is about one foot off the floor before striking it. In the pick-up you should strike the ball immediately as it rebounds off the floor.

When the ball is hit too hard or high, it will rebound off the back wall and will usually result in an easy kill shot for the advanced player. Very few players use a straight shot to the front wall for a kill from a back wall recovery unless they have the shot perfected. Instead, it is better to hit at least one other wall before hitting the front wall in order to avoid a possible easy setup and to make following the ball more difficult. When the ball rebounds with great force off the back wall, you should respond by hitting the kill shot from a position close to the short line, thus making it easier for you to control and to place. A ceiling shot which rebounds from the back wall at least as high as your knees will also become an easy setup for a kill shot. It is executed as previously described for a kill shot but requires much faster timing because of the sharper decline when the ball rebounds off the wall. Because of this angle, the swing is shorter whenever the ball is close to the back wall; indeed, at times the wrist snap is all that can be used.

Although not used too frequently, a kill shot is sometimes executed with an overhand stroke. In such situations the ball usually rebounds high off the floor; consequently it is used only when your opponent is in deep back court. The *overhand kill* can be hit on the fly or off a high bounce and should be directed to the corners.

The Ceiling Shot—When hitting a ceiling shot from the back court many better players use an underhand stroke in order to get a sharper angle and thus help prevent the ball from rebounding off the back wall. The ball should be hit with an open or slightly cupped hand to help guarantee greater control. It must be hit in the correct direction and with ample speed so that it strikes the ceiling close to the front wall, and in rebounding off the front wall and floor will carry to the back corner without permitting any back or side wall play.

Punch Ball Hit—In executing the ceiling shot, the passing shot, and at times the kill shot, you may use a *fist* or *punch ball hit*. To execute this shot your fingers should be tightly curled across the palm of your hand so that the middle bones of the fingers are almost flush with the heel of the hand. Your thumb should be placed alongside the index finger and should not cross the knuckles as is the fist used in boxing. An underhand or sidearm stroke should be used in hitting the ball and contact should be made at the junction of the knuckles and palm of your hand. Great speed can be gained with this hit as the bony surface of the fingers does not allow the ball to be cushioned as it is when hit from the palm or at the base of the fingers. Because of the greater speed given to the ball in this hit, the fist ball is used most often in a passing shot or when trying to get your opponent out of front court position. At times the ball may be hit directly at your opponent. The great speed will not permit him to get ready for the return and will prevent him from getting into position for a good return, especially if he is close to the front wall.

The fist ball can be used both offensively or defensively but is used predominantly as a defensive shot because it is difficult to control the ball. This may be understood when you realize that the hitting area is much smaller and the more irregular surface of the fingers does not allow for the accuracy which can be gained with the open or cupped hand. This hit is effective when you must play your weak hand in order to gain additional speed and when control is not a major factor.

The Passing Shot—An effective passing shot is one that seemingly hugs the side wall. Tremendous control is required to hit the ball to the front wall so that it angles off parallel to the side wall. You should strike the ball with an open hand, wrist cocked but flexed at the last second to help impart some side spin so the ball will come out at a straighter angle and remain close to the side wall. If your opponent anticipates this shot you should be able to change your swing quickly and direct the ball to the opposite side. This shot is especially impressive when your opponent runs back expecting the ball to rebound off the side wall only to see it pass a few feet away from his position.

Additional Hints

As improvement continues you should emphasize development of the weak arm until it can be used as effectively as the strong arm. The use of both arms will enable you to have better front-wall control because of the greater variety of shots and strokes thus made possible. By being in front court position, you will force your opponents to hit to you which helps set up the kill shot.

When playing a fast hard game, you should not overstretch to get a shot off but try instead to take an extra step in order to get you into a position where you can put more power and control into the shot. Many tall players have a tendency to overstretch because of their long reach but this should be avoided. Although a fast ball is an asset in a hard, fast moving game you should also be aware that speed without control is of little value.

There are still other shots and skills that you can employ but many of these are more individual preference than what can be termed basic elements. For example, when playing a high rebound off the back wall, you could stay close to the back wall and hit a ceiling shot with the overhand stroke. Also, what appears to be a certain shot at times may turn out to be a completely different one. For example, when you are ready to hit a ceiling shot and see your opponent move to the rear court in anticipation of the return, you should come down on the ball with the overhand stroke and execute a kill shot. The use of this and other shots depends upon the strategy being employed and upon which shots you can perform most successfully under existing circumstances.

Patterns of Play   6

Strategy for Singles Play

One of the best ways to begin developing your pattern of play is to think in terms of court position and whether you are on the offense or defense. You should always try to hold a position in the center of the court or on an imaginary line running through the center of the floor from front to back. This is the most advantageous position, for you can play to either side by taking a step or two or you can move up or back as the situation demands.

If this position is maintained your chances of being caught out of position will be very slim. Your opponent will be taxed in trying to get the ball away from you. Be ready to move in any direction. After hitting a shot move back into position immediately. Do not wait to see where your shot went or relax because it looked like a sure point. Once back into position you will again be in the most advantageous area for a return and usually will have time to think in terms of the next shot or how to retrieve the ball most effectively. If you are not in the correct position, your opponent will be able to hit the ball away from you; you will find yourself constantly running after the ball with little chance of returning it.

Being on the center line in front court is also very important as you do not look back to see where your opponent is hitting the ball. Keeping your eyes focused on the front wall, you should try to pick up the ball with peripheral vision and make the necessary move accordingly. You should also learn to listen for sounds in order to anticipate where your opponent is and to listen for the exact moment of the hit in order to prepare for the ball. By utilizing your senses, you can often determine in advance what to expect and from where to expect it.

The position you take on the court depends greatly on the shots that your opponent is using. If your opponent, for example, is always trying to kill the ball, you should position yourself a little closer to the front wall, just inside the short line. If he constantly tries to pass you, you should stand a little deeper in the court, one or two feet behind the short line. You will then be in a better receiving position and be able to make more returns with greater effectiveness. You should try to get in front of your opponent in the front and front center court position; by doing this, you are in a better position to return crucial kill shots and to execute the kill and passing shots. In essence, you can control the front wall; this is very important for scoring.

You should work to develop both a strong offense and a strong defense. When on the offensive, try to go for the kill or for a put away, and when on the defensive try to keep the ball in play until your opponent commits an error or until you can regain the offensive position. Most court play consists of a struggle to gain the center court position which is considered the offensive position. The main objective is to secure and maintain this position with offensive shots forcing your opponent to be on the move constantly while you direct the play. In order to retain this position it is necessary to keep your opponent in the back court or at least behind you; to accomplish this, use deep shots such as the passing or ceiling shot. A rally usually does not last long; so you should try for a put away as soon as the opportunity arises. This is most easily accomplished by getting your opponent out of position and then placing the next shot so that he will be unable to reach it or to play it well.

The server has the advantage in attaining center court position. This is why it is so important to have a good serve. If you serve weakly, your opponent can very easily put you on the defensive with a strong return. The main objective of the service therefore should be to score an ace or at least to force your opponent into a weak return. To be in the best position for the service return, you should get in the center of the court approximately one to two feet behind the short line. Without an effective serve or by not attaining proper position, the server will quickly lose the offense and be put on the defense.

The possibility of scoring an ace or forcing your opponent to hit a weak return depends to a great extent upon your opponent's weaknesses. You therefore should analyze your opponent's strokes and shots when you are warming up with him, before starting the game. You should determine at which height, with what speed, and in which direction you should hit the ball in order to secure the most effective results. If you notice that your opponent has trouble with his left arm, you should serve to the left side; if he has trouble with his overhead strokes, you should hit high shots to the corners; and if he has trouble handling hard hit balls, you should use the power shots. Analyzation should not stop after the game begins but should be continued so that you can constantly readjust your shots in terms of weaknesses discovered. This is a fundamental rule in handball: always play to your opponent's weak points and never play to his strong points, except occasionally to keep him from expecting the ball on the same side at all times.

If you are on the defense and wish to go on the offense, you must drive your opponent out of center court position into the back court. To do this you should use a passing shot, a lob, or a ceiling shot. Be careful not to hit the ball at such an angle that it will rebound straight off the back wall for this can result in an easy kill or pass setup. As the receiver of the service your most advantageous position is approximately five to six feet from the wall. From this position you can move in any direction to return the ball and force the server to move out of his controlling position. You should think of the return of service as one of the most important shots of the game.

Can you return most shots when the ball rebounds off the back wall at great speed? when the ball comes out at a sharp angle from the rear corner? when the ball stays close to the rear wall or rear side wall?

The importance of using a variety of serves can be demonstrated. If the server consistently hits to one side, the receiver should stand more to that side, neutralizing the effectiveness of the serve by shortening the amount of time necessary to get to the ball and by being prepared for the serve before it is hit. Such anticipation is not possible unless your opponent consistently uses the same serve. The good player will not fall into the habit of hitting the same shots or serves over and over. Habitual actions are soon capitalized on. It is important to have a large repertoire of shots and not to rely solely on a few strong shots.

As an offensive player it is important to keep your opponent off stride; so he cannot get set for an effective return which would drive you out of center court position. This can be achieved if you play every shot with a definite plan, placing it in a particular spot. Aimless return of the ball keeps you in trouble and will not contribute to the development of skill or strategy. Use different shots, change pace, and make different placements. In this way you will keep your opponent off balance and make him play to your advantage. As an example, a soft, easy shot after a rally of hard-hit fast moving balls is usually sufficient to throw your timing off even if you are a top level player. In placing the ball you should try the following effective hits: low at your opponent's feet; hard and fast, directly at him when very close to the front wall; close to the side wall so that he will be hesitant to take a full swing; rebounds off one or two side walls so the ball will not come straight out and to put spin on the ball.

The important factors in keeping the offensive are to be aggressive and to have confidence in your ability. If you begin to fret over certain shots or become flustered when you are being beaten, your chances of losing the game are greatly increased. You have undoubtedly seen or heard of an athlete who beat himself; this is usually due to his inability to cope with situations—a bad play on his part, or a spectacular play made by his opponent. Under these circumstances this player may begin to press his shots only to find that instead of improving, his game becomes progressively worse. You should, in such situations, force yourself to relax and take more time on your shots and placements. You will then begin to hit the ball effectively; this in turn will help you to regain your confidence.

Aggressiveness is a quality that must be developed for it will cause your opponent to press his game and it can be the deciding factor in your game. To be aggressive you should try for every shot. There is not a shot, except for a kill roll out, that cannot be returned if you can reach it. Positioning therefore is very important. If you are trying to return a well executed shot, you may have to resort to still other measures to get to the ball. These may include diving after a kill shot, leaping for a high ball, or climbing the walls to avoid banging into a wall on a sharp fast break to the sides. In all cases try for every shot; do not let any shots go by uncontested even when you think there is no chance for a return. You will probably amaze yourself when you see how many balls you return by doing this; it will help increase your confidence and shatter your opponent's.

When you are losing, it is usually a good idea to change your style of play. For example, if you have been trying for a kill on every shot, go for more passing or ceiling shots. If you have been using a power type game, go for more control and easy placements with lobs and ceiling shots. If you find that you are having difficulty with a certain shot, do not try it for a few points and pick it up later if warranted. If you are playing a winning game, maintain the same style. If you possess a sufficiently great margin, however, it is a good idea to experiment with new or different innovations but still keep the same basic game.

One of the main objectives of four-wall handball is to keep your opponent on the run and to force him to take difficult shots. This is true on all skill levels but it becomes decreasingly important as your skill improves. For the very advanced player there are few very hard shots and it is almost impossible to keep your opponent constantly on the run. The level of skill is so high that execution of one shot can completely change the picture of play, and the game becomes a battle of the minds rather than one of strength and speed.

To play on this level takes maturation which is at least partially the result of practice and play on all levels of competition. You should begin to develop the ability to anticipate, to think ahead, to make quick decisions, and be able to analyze your game and your opponent's game. The more you play a thoughtful game, the more improvement you will see in your tactics and all around ability to play. You will also be winning many more games and developing greater confidence in yourself.

Many cases can be cited as examples of anticipation, thinking ahead, last minute decision making, and player analyzation. An obvious example is when you feint your opponent into hitting the ball where you want it by making a definite move in one direction but then immediately reversing as your opponent makes his hit. The hitter in this situation will be trying to hit away from you and will hit in the opposite direction of your feint. If you want to fake your opponent out of position, you should set yourself as in making a definite shot. Then as your opponent anticipates the shot and moves to position himself for it, you should hit the ball at a different angle at the last possible moment. When your opponent is caught out of position on one side of the court, he will expect the ball down the opposite side; and as he makes his move, hit the ball to the side where he was originally positioned. Whenever your opponent is set in good position for an expected kill shot, you should hit an easy high shot or ceiling shot to the back court.

In executing the kill shot do not try to roll it out but take into consideration your opponent's position in the court, his physical condition, and the score of the game. If the score is well in your favor and your opponent is very fast, you should go for a low, flat kill to avoid any possible return. When your opponent is caught in deep back court and is not very fast, you should hit a relatively high, safe kill or a soft kill to avoid any chance of error.

If you are alert and in good position, any other equally effective plays can be made merely by catching mistakes made by your opponent. For example, if on an attempted ceiling shot the ball does not hit the ceiling but hits the front wall first, a fly-kill setup or an easy, back-wall setup may arise. If a ceiling shot is angled too sharply, the ball may hit the side wall on the rebound off the floor and become an easy setup for a kill or passing shot. It is only by observing your opponent and his shots that you can take advantage of his mistakes and anticipate the shot in time for proper positioning. There are many possibilities that arise and each must be resolved at the moment it happens if the end result is to be in your favor. Thus it is important to think of what you will do when a certain situation presents itself before it occurs. This is usually done whenever there is a lull in the game, between rallies, or during time outs. Do not be hesitant to talk to yourself during the game as it will help keep you relaxed and attuned to what should be done in a certain situation.

Strategy for Doubles Play

Most of the preceding descriptions of play and the various strategies used are also applicable to the game of doubles. Because of the addition of two more players, the court is usually much better covered and requires greater accuracy in placements. Even more important is the teamwork that is developed by each team, for you must share responsibilities in covering the court and in determining who is to take various hits when both have an opportunity to return the ball.

The best doubles teams are not always composed of the best singles players but more often are developed when each partner complements the other in terms of the strong hand, physical abilities, strongest shots, type of play, and other factors. If the strong points of one partner make up for the weak points of the other, the combination will usually be quite effective and successful. Two top singles players usually have a tendency to play a singles game and take many shots which should be played by the other partner. It is possible to develop a strong doubles team by constantly practicing together so that each partner knows instinctively which ball he should play and can anticipate his partner's actions. Before beginning play each team should decide, through analyzation of their strong and weak points, which side they should play. The player with the stronger left arm should play the left side in order to cover this side most effectively and the stronger right arm, the right side.

To define court responsibilities you should divide the court in such a manner that a definite playing arrangement can be exercised. The main objective of any arrangement should be to play side by side in front court position so that no balls can get by. Remember that when you are up front, you are on offense; and if you drop back to the rear court, you are on defense. So important is this front position that you should try to take every ball that comes your way and to return it as effectively as possible in order to keep your front court position and to keep your opponents in the back court. If this position can be maintained, it will not be long before you get a chance for a kill shot which will end the rally. In this position the left-side player should take most balls in the middle court because of his strong right arm. All balls hit to the back court or balls hit at a sharp angle of rebound off the front and side walls should be taken by the player on the side toward which the ball is travelling.

If both players were to take all the shots hit on the side on which they were positioned, they would soon find themselves out of position and vulnerable for a put away. If the left-side player, for example, tried to return all balls coming out of the left-hand corner, he would have to run into the right side of the court, thus leaving the left side unguarded. The same would apply to the right-side player who tries to return all balls coming out of the right corner. In addition, he would be using his weak left arm for many shots. Sharply hit angle shots off the front wall should be allowed to rebound off the side wall if hit sufficiently high and taken by the player on the opposite side. (See Figure 8.)

When playing side by side, it is imperative that each player cover for his partner whenever he is caught out of position. Thus, if your partner is caught in the back court, be prepared for a quick return volley to the front court on his side. If anticipated in time you can then hit a slow lob or corner ceiling shot to drive your opponent back and give your partner ample time to get back into position. Since it is not always possible to cover well in such situations, it makes it imperative for the player who is in the back court to immediately come up to his front court position after returning the ball. The best position in doubles is for each partner to stand just back of the short line equidistant from the other and from the side wall. This is a little closer than in singles but it is necessary in order to return all low hit balls to the front court and, at the same time through alert coverage of each partner, to cover the back court. Because of this close front court position, a hard fast drive at your opponent's feet can prove very effective as there is less time for him to maneuver into the proper position. A well-placed shot can also be used for passing purposes whenever it is hit very hard.

Rallies in a game of doubles are usually longer than in singles because of better court coverage and this makes it difficult to hit a shot that cannot be returned. Most shots will be defensive, whether they be hit up front or in the back court, until an opportunity occurs to use an offensive shot. This makes it necessary for you always to think ahead one or two shots, working to get your opponent out of position or to make a mistake so that you can come in with a kill.

Since these offensive opportunities occur less frequently in doubles, you should always be on the alert to observe and capitalize on them. To help elicit these mistakes or to out maneuver your opponents, you must, as in singles, analyze both of your opponents' possible weaknesses. When it is determined who has less ability or is weak in certain shots, you should relay this information to your partner and then both of you should concentrate your attack on these weaknesses.

Many top doubles teams (both right-handed) prefer an arrangement in which the right-side player covers the front court and that area included to the right of an imaginary line drawn from the left-hand corner to the

FRONT WALL   FRONT WALL

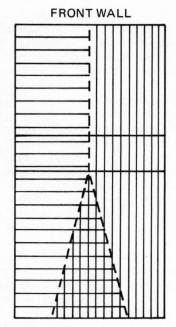
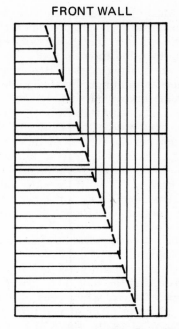

Figure 8—Court coverage. ▤   *Figure 9—Court coverage.* ▤
Area covered by left-side play-   *Area covered by left-side play-*
er. ‖‖‖ *Area covered by right-*   *er.* ‖‖‖ *Area covered by right-*
side player. ▦ *Area covered*   *side player.*
by either player depending
upon the shot.

rear right-hand corner. (See Figure 9.) If the ball is high when coming out
of the left-hand corner, the right-side player should let it rebound off the
right-side wall so that his partner can take it from a better position with
his right hand. The left-side player should take all balls hit a few feet high
out of the right-hand corner; so the strong arm can once again be used.
With this cross-balance coverage it can be seen how difficult it is to hit
kill shots in the front court. The right-side player must, however, be very
skilled in the kill shot while the left-side player must be highly skilled in
back-wall play and in his ability to cover the court, for usually most shots
are directed to him.

If a team is composed of a right-handed player and a left-handed
player, the left-handed player should play the left side and the right-handed
the right side. Such a combination is very strong on side-wall shots because
of the strong arms on each side. If playing against such a team you should
direct many returns down the middle between the players so that they have
to use their weak arms. It usually is rare, however, when a player cannot
return a ball hit down the middle.

Most of the serves used in singles are not equally effective in doubles, because the receivers are much closer to the corners. Receivers should be positioned as in singles but with each partner side by side, equidistant from each other and the side walls. The most effective serves therefore are those that are sharply angled, that bounce at the receiver's feet, or go into the corners for an unpredictable angle of rebound. To increase the effectiveness of your serves you should fake the direction of your serves, use different speeds, and vary the kinds of serves. You should also serve from the center or on your side of the center of the service zone in order to be in proper position for the return. At times the position of the receivers will help you in determining which serve to use. For example, if the receivers stand close to the short line and continually try to volley the serve, you should hit the ball hard and low off the side wall. You may also elect to hit a corner shot to drive them back, but it must be sufficiently high so they cannot volley it. An occasional cross-court serve is also effective as is an easy, high shot very close to the side wall where your opponents will not be able to return the ball with any degree of accuracy or power.

Each player should play every shot and at the same time be ready to remain in or attain good defensive position as soon as he sees that his partner is taking the shot. This "cover" of your partner will pay many dividends as, for example, when your partner decides at the last moment to let the ball go by in favor of you or if by chance he misses the shot. When one player receives the serve, the other should quickly move up to the front court for defense as should the receiver after hitting the ball.

Players should always talk to each other during and after a hand-out or point. During play, the talk should consist mainly of indicating the taking of shots by calling "mine" or "yours." Talk should be short and concise. It is also good practice to give words of praise such as "good shot" or "good cover" as this helps keep up morale and confidence. Words of encouragement should also be given when needed. This should be done when the ball is dead or not in play so that you will not hold up the game. A team is very hard to beat if each player knows that his partner has faith and confidence in him.

It should be mentioned here that there are some players who think it is good strategy to "stretch" the rules. This occurs when on an easy back wall setup your opponent purposely positions himself in a direct line with your shot so that it will hit him for a hinder which calls for a replay. This practice should be avoided at all times as, aside from being illegal, it defeats the basic premise of the game: each player should have an unobstructed view and shot at the ball and there should be no interference with the shot.

Rules of the Game 7

The following is not a duplication of the rules, as copies of official rules can easily be secured in most sporting goods stores and wherever handball is played. There are, however, basic knowledges and explanations which are necessary for playing a high-level game. Other than in a championship match, seldom are there referees present during play; consequently responsibility for legal play rests with the participants. It is important, therefore, that you have good understanding of the rules so that you can recognize infractions and enact the appropriate penalties.

Playing Regulations

To decide who serves first in a regulation match a coin is tossed. When there is no referee present, various other methods may be employed: a rebound toss to the short line or back wall or other similar methods. You must start and complete the serve from anywhere in the service zone which is bounded by the short line and the service line (a line running parallel to the short line five feet closer to the front wall). Stepping on the lines is permissable but if you step over a line in the act of serving this is a *fault*. Two such faults constitute an *out* (hand-out or side-out). To serve you drop the ball on the floor and then strike it on its first bounce from the floor. If you attempt to hit the ball and fail to do so, you are out, as you also are if you bounce the ball more than three times in the service zone before serving—before contacting the ball. Before serving the ball, you should be sure that your opponent is ready. If you quick serve, the point should be replayed without penalty. You may request a time-out after a point or hand-out in order to wipe your glasses, face, or to take care of any other necessary detail. The time-out must not exceed 30 seconds, however, and not more than three time-outs are granted to each player or side in a game.

To serve legally, the ball must pass the short line before it can be returned. This prevents the receiver from charging the ball as soon as it is hit by the server. If your served ball fails to bounce on the floor behind the short line, this is termed a *short* and must be replayed. Two consecutive shorts constitute an out in which case your opponent then becomes the server. Also included in the illegal category are those serves which hit the ceiling, back wall, or two side walls before hitting the floor behind the short line. An illegally served ball may not be played and must be re-served unless it is the second such short serve, in which case it is an out.

On the service and during play, the ball should be dry and any violation of this rule results in forfeiture of the serve. When wet, additional spin can be put on the ball; this results in an unfair advantage analogous to that witnessed in baseball with the spitball. In a match the referee may put a new ball in play if the ball is wet, or require you to change your gloves if they are too wet.

In doubles, the server's partner must stand within the service box with his back to the wall and with both feet on the floor until the ball passes the short line. In this way he does not interfere with the receiver's vision or gain unfair advantage by getting into position early. If your partner is hit by a served fly ball while standing in the service box, this counts as a *dead ball* without penalty, but does not eliminate any short or fault preceding this serve. If your partner is hit by the served ball on the bounce, it is a short ball. If he moves out of the service box in order to avoid being hit by the served ball, this constitutes a violation. If hit during such movement, he is penalized by an out and the ball is automatically dead. When the served ball passes behind your partner and strikes the floor behind the short line, it is a dead ball but does not eliminate a short preceding this serve. Many times the ball may pass behind your partner when he flexes his knees, head, or trunk in order to avoid being hit; but if his feet are on the ground and his back is to the side wall, no penalty is incurred.

As a receiver you must stand at least five feet back of the short line while the ball is being served. You are required to play a legal serve either on the fly or on the first bounce. Whenever there is an illegal service, play immediately stops and voids any play of the ball that may follow. To eliminate any misunderstanding you should not catch or stop, in any way, an illegally served ball, even if it looks obvious.

During play if the ball is swung at and missed, you or your partner may continue your attempt to again play the ball before the second bounce. This occurs occasionally when you miss an attempt on a hard-hit ball in mid-court but you can still play the ball upon its rebound off the back wall. Many times your opponent may be behind you in such situations, and if he is hit by the ball after you miss in your attempt, it counts against him—either a point or hand-out as the case may be.

If you are unintentionally interfered with by your opponent in your attempt to run to the back wall for the second try, this is termed a *hinder* and must be replayed. As the term implies, hinder refers to interference. A hinder also occurs when a returned ball hits your opponent before striking the floor, even if the ball continues to the front wall or was traveling toward the back wall. In this case, as in all legal unintentional hinders, the ball is dead and must be replayed. Other frequent hinders occur whenever you unintentionally interfere with your opponent, thus preventing him from having a fair chance to return the ball. To avoid causing such hinders you should always move out of the way of the oncoming ball toward the front wall. Your movement should always be toward the center of the court so that you do not get caught with your back up against the side wall only to watch the ball go by when you are out of position. In a regulation match the referee is empowered to call a hinder, but when there is no referee present, the call becomes your responsibility.

Decisions regarding hinders should be liberal; so as to discourage any practice of playing the ball where your adversary cannot see it until too late to prepare for the hit. It is no excuse to say that the ball was killed or that your opponent could not get to it, for each player is entitled to a fair chance to recover the ball. This rule is abused by players who think that it would be a weak excuse to have the play repeated. They feel that as long as you can get your hand on the ball it should be played and only when you make physical contact with your opponent, preventing him from reaching the ball or executing a swing, should a hinder be called. This is in opposition to the main intent of the game and should be avoided as much as possible. In doubles, if you are interfered with by your partner it is not a hinder. Hinders can occur only between you and your opponent.

If the ball passes between your legs, a *straddled ball*, this is sometimes considered a hinder. The decision depends upon whether the ball was obscured from sight or the action interfered with following the flight of the ball. This occurs when you jump up or split your legs to avoid getting hit by the ball, especially when close to the front wall. In the case of a *screen ball*, when the legally served ball returns from the front wall so close to the server that he obstructs your view of the ball, the ball is immediately dead and should be replayed. It does not void any previous short ball.

Remember that it is the duty of the side that has played the ball to get out of the way of the opponents. You cannot just hold your position after the hit or move in any direction, even if it is to gain center court position, so that view of the ball or the play by your opponent is obstructed. In such cases an avoidable hinder occurs; this is also known as the *hinder point* or out, depending upon whether the offender was receiving or serving. Avoidable hinders occur when you move into a position effecting a block; when you do not move sufficiently to allow your opponent his shot; or move in the way of, and are struck by the ball just played by your opponent. For example, let us assume that your opponent hits a weak shot that comes straight off the back wall for what seems to be an easy return for a kill or passing shot. He then moves a few feet behind the short line and places himself directly in the line of your hit so that when you hit the ball it will strike him in the back.

Care should be exercised in calling an unavoidable hinder as many times what looks like an unavoidable hinder is purely unintentional. The deciding factor should be whether or not your opponent made some attempt to get out of your way even though it was relatively impossible to do so. If the court in which you are playing has obstructions such as door latches, indented windows, protruding lights or air ducts, which when contacted by the ball cause it to rebound in an abnormal manner, this is a court hinder. There is no penalty on such a hinder and the play involving that point must be done over.

From the foregoing it can be seen that the rules governing handball are straightforward; they do not require lengthy explanations and/or interpretations. This is one of the reasons why handball is so enjoyable. It is very simple to play but a top level game requires the highest degree of skill.

8 Unwritten Laws

To make the game of handball most enjoyable there are certain unwritten rules and traditions which you should abide by. Because of the close quarters and the intimacy of play, it is necessary to exemplify the highest ideals of sportsmanship in order to enjoy a smooth and uncontested game.

As in most other sports, if you do not know your opponent, you should introduce yourself at the beginning of play and let him know your caliber of play. If you are a beginner and he is a class A player, it would not be fair to him if you played, as you would not be able to give him a game. In such a case he may then find another player more equal in ability and you would do likewise. Unless there are extenuating circumstances, however, most players do not consider themselves so good that they refuse to play either with or against a poorer player as long as it is within reasonable limits. For most effective and worthwhile play both players should be of about the same ability. It takes very little time to discover the truth of a "verbal game" once play begins.

As handball requires much deep concentration and anticipation it is important that you not talk unnecessarily during a rally or between plays. There is nothing more infuriating to a player than to have his thinking disrupted by constant chattering. This does not mean that you should be completely silent throughout a game for there are many times when a few words are called for or needed. It is proper, for example, to compliment your opponent when he makes a very good shot or *dig*, a return of a ball that appeared to be impossible to return. Politeness indicates that you recognize skilled play; complimenting your opponent shows your respect and admiration. Recognition of your opponent's good play shows good sportsmanship. Spectators should behave in the same manner.

Whenever a serious question arises during play, you should give your honest opinion regarding the point in question. If it is not possible to come to a conclusion, you should agree to play the point over. Many times your opponent may be in a position where he cannot see your hit or the outcome of your shot. It is therefore necessary for you to call the play as soon as it happens. This may occur often on a dig where it is difficult to ascertain whether the return was made off the first or second bounce. Sometimes it is hard to determine if a kill shot hits the floor before hitting the front wall.

Team B is the receiver. Which player should return the serve when it follows the paths indicated by 1 and 2? In each case, why should this player return the ball and which arm should he use? If player B hit a ball which traveled as indicated by path 2 what should Team A do from the positions shown?

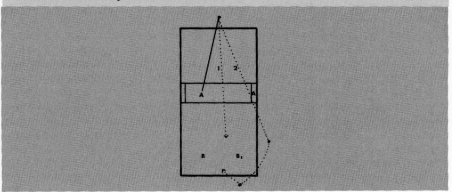

If your opponent expresses or shows any doubt regarding the legitimacy of the play, the point should be replayed. If your opponent calls the shot and is in the most advantageous position to do so, you should accept his decision without question.

During play, you should call all illegal hits as, for example, when you hit the ball on your wrist, arm, or with a double hit. Many times such hits can be recognized if the ball takes off in an unexpected flight or can be determined by the sound produced by the hit. If the game has been in progress for any length of time, illegal contact will result in a wet ball, from perspiration. Discovery of a wet ball after a supposedly good hit is quite disconcerting and leads to disrespect.

You should always examine the ball to see if it is wet before serving. If it is, dry it; wipe the ball with a dry portion of your clothing, with a towel or by rolling the ball on the floor under your foot. Before putting the ball into play, you should then let your opponent examine it so that it meets with his satisfaction. This practice is very important when playing under very hot or humid conditions. You should wear a light cotton shirt to absorb perspiration and to help prevent accidents which may occur if perspiration gets on the floor.

One of the most exacting phases of play requiring high level sportsmanship is that associated with the calling of hinders. You may have a tendency to play it safe and not call a hinder so that your opponent will not think you are taking advantage by cancelling what may have been a good shot. A general rule of thumb that can be used in such a case is this: if your opponent legitimately interfered with your shot, either by being too close to you or by obstructing your view of the ball, you should call a hinder. More important is that you should always attempt, honestly, not to interfere with the person trying for a return. You should move out of his way so that he can follow the ball and be able to execute his stroke, even if it sometimes means giving up a strategic position. Only in this way can there be fewer hinders called; this means that you will enjoy a faster and cleaner game. This is especially true in doubles, for in this case the chances for having hinders are twice as many.

You should call a hinder only when you are involved in the play. You should not be in the back court and call a hinder when your opponent makes a kill from front court position for you could not follow the play all the way and would have no possible chance of returning the ball. Nor should it be necessary for you to make body contact with your opponent to prove that you could not execute a shot or reach the ball. You should respect your opponent's decisions and if there is serious doubt there should be a discussion of the rules in order to clarify any misunderstanding. Most handball players display admirable integrity in abiding by the rules, thus enabling them to play excellent games without the services of a referee. Good players do not look for ways to circumvent the rules so that they can gain a point or two.

During certain hours of the day when handball courts are in full use, it is sometimes necessary to limit the amount of playing time. In such cases it is customary to let the team playing finish its game even if by so doing your own reserved playing time is shortened. When the following team arrives you should limit your game by lowering the points needed to decide a winner. In this way you can complete your game and not take more than a few minutes of the following team's time.

When playing a friendly courteous game, you should alternate your serves to either side when playing singles and to alternate receivers when playing doubles. In this way there is equal opportunity to play strong and weak shots.

Play hard but play fairly. If you want to be respected, never resort to unfair tactics.

Index